JOURNEY INTO Wholeness

A Devotional Journal for Intentional Authentic Living

Betty W. Williams, D. Min., LMFT

Printed in the United States of America.

First Printed August 1st, 2023

ISBN: 978-1-956544-53-4

Printed by Amazon.com

www.BetweenFriendsPublishing.com

This book is dedicated to my enduring husband who sometimes wanted me to make more money instead of words. Thank you for your patient love, gentle shoves, and incredible support through the ups, downs, crooks, and turns of the journey. May the wisdom that we have shared and garnered be a blessing to those who read and desire transformation in their journeys.

Table of Contents

Introduction

I like thinking of life in terms of a journey. It reminds me that change is inevitable. There is a new adventure every day. However, living in a way that makes positive and lasting impact takes intentionality. This involves authentic living. Authentic living means living in the present with the awareness of the past and future. It also means being aware of all the different parts of self: intellectual, emotional, physical, social, and spiritual. The intellectual part of us knows what it means to pick apart a problem and come up with a solution. The emotional part of us wants to acknowledge the pain or happiness that is experienced hourly. We know we can't live off of these emotions, but we certainly can't bury them either. The physical part of us is the easiest to identify. It is the part that others see, feel, and judge. Our body shape, our hair color and style, eye color, skin color, and how we get around in the world are all part of our physical being. The social piece is about how we connect to others. Being an introvert versus an extrovert can have different advantages depending on time and place. Spirituality is a little harder to unpack. This has to do with how one connects to God and the concepts that are bigger than what one can always see or feel. Religion tries to provide some concreteness to our spiritual understandings.

Authenticity is about being aware of how I think, feel, and go about in the world without trying to pretend that I am not who or what I am. It means that I am willing to look at me and the world with eyes wide open. It means that while being aware of my good and bad traits, I am willing and wanting to change into my best self. This is risky because one has to have an open heart with an awareness that pain is a part of the process. However, revelation is a beautiful thing! I know from experience that when I am at my best authentic self, there is a wholeness that exudes peace.

Most of us only achieve this for short periods of time. As stated earlier, it takes great intentionality with discipline. It becomes somewhat easier the older we get because we learn a great deal on the journey of living. Still, in this post-modern era in this country, it is easy to become fragmented by the many voices calling to us from many different corners. In this digital age there are twenty-four-hour experts who are telling us how we should live. There are the expectations of family members and deadlines of our jobs. There are our religious connections and our friends who want to and should provide some accountability.

We all know what fragmentation feels or looks like. It is that overwhelmed feeling, that I just can't get it together state of mind, that I can't even find my socks or car keys kind of day. It is that interaction in which you heard what was said but you have no idea what was meant. It is those hours you spend doing lots of things but get nothing done. It is that driving around for days and getting nowhere. The deeper more lasting question is: How do I want to live and am I living it? Another important question is: Does it matter?

I am writing this book because deep down we all know that it really does even if we didn't have the research and experts telling us how much it does matter. The stress of feeling pulled in too many places by too many things cannot net good results for any individual or group. As a counselor, I have spent many years helping people find the pieces of themselves. As a chaplain, I've been present with others as they experienced the miraculous peace that comes from spiritual connection. As a teacher, I have spent many years studying and learning with students because I am in love with the idea that embodied knowledge transforms. If ever there was a time when we need all of the above (de-fragmentation, miraculous peace, and transformation), it is now. In a world of self-violence, unprovoked violence to others, divisions based on otherness, and materialism as god, surely striving for authentic wholeness can net something.

I get that on different days in different settings one can be different with different people. However, the problem comes when one forgets or loses the original identity. The core character and personality should be able to expand and contract without losing originality. There are some experts who say that it is impossible to lose one's original personality. This may be true but I have experienced and seen/heard too many people who have experienced this phenomenon of fragmented loss of self. Staying in tune to one's God identity while being present in loving others unconditionally is a gift and a discipline.

In the pages that follow you will find my notes about authentic whole living that have come from counseling, teaching, and spiritual attention to others. I have put them in story form to make them more practical. The stories are a part of my story. For the sake of de-identification and privacy, the people are conglomerates of people that I have met along the way. They are not necessarily one person in particular. The hope is that you will find them helpful in defragmenting your world. This means reading each story in a quiet space and allowing it to speak to you. The goal is that the focus will not be so much as what this writer is teaching you but what you might learn from these encounters. The best client is not one who emulates the counselor but glens wisdom from the process and is open to transformation. Look for clues from the title of the chapters as a path of meditation. At the end of each story, I have added an exercise to help you capture the authenticity at your moment of reading. It is my hope that you will engage the text though some suggestions may feel a little risky. This is a way that my notes can help you fill in your story.

Chapter One

Stretching Your Identity

I can still hear the cadence of the drum and the loud guttural chattering sounds coming from the crowd. The van rounded the curve and cleared the jungle of trees. We found ourselves in a clearing full of unfamiliar dark faces. Some were painted, some frowned, and some were smiling. They were yelling a rhythmic language that was unintelligible to us in perfect unison. The drumbeats were coming from somewhere. I'm not sure if it was feet or some type of instrument, but it seemed deafening. It was frightening yet intriguing. Our hosts did not seem to be afraid so this gave us courage. The bodies, some naked, some wearing bright colored clothing ran with the van until it came to a stop. We were in a jungle in Africa. It was still hard to believe, but it somehow seemed that we had been there before.

My husband and I, along with several others, were there supposedly on a mission to teach, mentor, and provide medical care. As always, we were the ones who had much to learn. The order of each day was to get dressed, pack supplies, and travel to the assignment for the day. There were plenty of obstacles which included the slow process of getting medicine from the clinic, the rainy season that included occasional downpours each day, lack of supplies including clean water, the daring drive through clogged traffic, driving on under-developed roads, the physical sickness that dogged our team, and the language barriers.

However, I couldn't shake the feeling that I knew these people; like somehow they were my kin. We even had a conversation one night with our host about what tribe we might belong to if we had been born in Liberia. He made this discernment by looking at our facial features. I think the familiarity came from being called Black or African American for much of my life. It was knowing that some of my ancestors really may have walked in this land at some point. The color of our skin was similar but they called us "shiny" Americans. However, they were also quick to call us brother, sister, or cousin.

Despite this, or maybe because of this, acclamation and enjoying the journey was tough. The hardest day was followed by breakthrough. On the first clinic day, the line of people looked like hundreds to our puny staff of seven or eight. Again, our progress was very slow and it was so hot we all felt like we were melting. The people patiently waited, sometimes standing for hours in tight spaces. My husband commented later with a grim face on the level of sickness we faced. He wasn't optimistic about some of the outcomes. I remember holding a tiny baby that was burning with fever and just standing and praying because I felt so helpless to change her world.

God was gracious and the next day we got reinforcement from a local hospital somewhere in the vicinity. We were able to get trained medical staff through a medical professional that was our host's relative. The second day was better but still long and hard with long lines. Because of the extra help, we were able to spend more time with the people. Our teachers spent time in classrooms and others milled around the crowd.

At some point in the afternoon after a rain shower, we decided to play some music. We were able to rig up a sound system so that it could be heard throughout the school grounds where we were hosting our makeshift clinic. We had a microphone so we could talk to the crowd. We were told that they could understand most of our English although we could understand very little of their dialects. I got my turn at the mic. I remember telling my story of being a little girl and dreaming of traveling to a distant land. Here I was in a distant land as an adult in a land of my ancestors. I encouraged them to continue to hope and dream. I don't remember my words, but felt the spiritual connection. The music started and without being coerced, the people began to dance. Dancing seemed like such a natural thing for them. There were only a few dancers at first, then others joined in. We, the team, just looked at them with curiosity. Their dance didn't have any choreography or particular style, but it did have rhythm. It also looked very *freeing*. I remember deciding to dance with them. It took a minute of deciding not to think too much about what others would think or how silly I might look, but eventually I decided to dance. I didn't begin with a sense of choreography. I just started to move. *It felt very freeing*.

There we were dancing together. People had gotten out of line or stopped whatever they were doing and came to the middle of the compound where the music was playing. We were just dancing together, the team and the people. For a few minutes we were one in the freedom of just moving to the music. I will never forget that day with my arms wide and my face to the sun dancing with my relatives of a distant land. It taught me so many lessons about identity, letting go, dancing despite the pain of life, and becoming one with others. Deciding to dance was risky, but it was actually symbolic of all the risk that it took to get on a plane, fly twenty-four hours, and open my heart to the adventure of something so unfamiliar yet familiar. I will forever remember the people who were suffering yet dared to dance in the face of that suffering. The dance that was not choregraphed or made up; it all came naturally. It was out of a soul that was open to the moment of stretching, believing, and becoming.

MEDITATIVE EXERCISE:

Take a few minutes to put on some music and just dance: No choreography expected or required. When you finish, write about what you feel and the memories that come up for you. What time in your life does it bring back for you? Are you still that person? How have you grown?

____

____

____

____

____

____

Chapter Two

The Naked Now: Living in Each Moment

The bed covers were rumpled and the room had an antiseptic spray smell. There were pictures on the surrounding tables, flowers, and a brightly wrapped basket of fruit. The man on the bed had a slight frown on his face and the family members present all looked like they were trying too hard to be cheerful. My patient was dying and everyone in the room knew it, but no one really wanted to talk about it. There were many reasons why that was. One, the weeks in the hospital watching his demise had been painful and fatiguing. Two, the sudden last words of the hospital medical staff that included hospice seemed too final and they were all trying to deal with the first level of loss. Three, the majority really wanted his final days or months to be filled with positivity and not tears and grief. There were a million other reasons in the room that had to do with individual relationships with the person dying. My goal was just to assess the patient and family to see how I might support them in the process. It was immediately evident that it was not the right time to ask a lot of probing questions. I introduced myself and purpose for being there to the patient and said that I would return later.

Later, the room was dark except for the light from the window. There was no other person present and the man had his eyes closed. Instrumental music came from the phone on the bedside table. He opened his eyes and attempted a smile when I came in. I again said who I was and my purpose for being there. After a quick review of his life, I found that he was an academic and a philosopher with a love of music and poetry. His wife had died several years prior and his children were adoringly close. They were all very educated with their own families and careers and issues, but still supported him very much. There were other family members and friends who came and went. We got to the spiritual piece of the assessment and he was noncommittal. He said that he had done the obedient, obligatory church thing but had been quite satisfied with not attending church for years. However, he was happy to talk about his poetry. I asked if I could stop in every now and then and read some with him. He agreed and thus was the beginning of a beautiful tutoring relationship.

Each Tuesday, depending on how he felt and number of visitors present, I would pull out the worn copy of his book. Some poems were about the sorrow of loss, not necessarily death, but loss in general, like the loss of a house, a friend, or a dream. His poetic words drew me in. The words were beautifully put together and the emotions were so powerful. I commented on this once. He said one of the most important things about life was in order to live free one must capture what one was feeling while feeling it. It was important to "Write It Down."

There were other poems that made me laugh out loud and some that seemed to carry an anxious sub-line. Yet each poem was refreshingly honest. So was my conversation with this man. He was refreshingly honest. On the days he was afraid he was honest about that emotion and told me why. On the days when he was feeling anxious, he said he was nervous, frustrated, and sometimes angry about many different things. He felt anger mostly about his disease process and his inability to do anything about it. He didn't blame God, but he certainly expressed some frustration about what God was doing. He wasn't afraid of death, but he didn't really want to leave his children and grandchildren behind. The days when he laughed or wore a quirky kind of smile were days that some of his favorite family members visited. Once someone brought a dog. That was the day he got up and walked outside in the sunshine for the first time in many days.

When the end was near, he couldn't talk as much, then not at all. He would drift off when I tried to read to him or never wake at all. When he was awake and there were close family members present, he would open his hand and the favorite ones knew they were to take it and hold it. The warmth of the touch obviously brought him some sense of relief or pleasure. I felt honored when one day I was the only one in the room and he stretched out his arm and opened his hand which I took. The warmth of his hand oddly brought a sense of relief and a peace that I knew that he knew that he was really dying. He was gone a day later.

I knew that I would be asked to speak at his funeral. I felt torn but knew that I had been given the gift of sharing his last days and needed to share what I learned. So I did. I wrote down the most important lessons that were learned in those days. They included the following: 1.) there is so much freedom in not being afraid to feel, 2.) carefree love is so much better than just loving, and 3.) spirituality is so much bigger than any religion could ever explain.

I was so drawn in by his ability to be so honest yet so loving and carefree. I've met very few people who embodied all three.

I always came away from visiting him feeling refreshed and not tired. He seemed to accept loss as just another part of life, even the loss of his own physical life.

MEDITATIVE EXERCISE:

Find a quiet space and allow no interruptions for a few minutes. Take a journal with you.

Try this breathing exercise: Slow down your breathing so that you are counting 1, 2, 3 with each inhale and exhale. Pay close attention to your breaths while telling yourself to relax. Feel the tension leave your body and relax.

After about ten minutes of relaxation, allow yourself to feel whatever comes up. Write down what you are feeling. Where do these emotions take you in your mind? Write it down.

____

____

____

____

____

____

____

Chapter Three

Standing in the Shoes of My Neighbor

They said the auditorium would hold at least five hundred people. It looked like every seat was filled. The music was playing an upbeat tempo and the speakers for the night were nervously pacing backstage. The air felt like electricity as the people chattered excitedly above the sounds of the small band on stage. I looked out at the crowded room of women, maybe a few children, from behind a stage curtain. I was part of an American team that had arrived in Moscow, Russia, the former Soviet Union, maybe twenty-four hours prior to this assembly. We were here as part of a delegation that was to do this encouraging conference for the women present. We represented several different American churches that were a part of one organization. We were told by our hosts and interpreters that the women were from as far as two hours away by car. The diversity in their economic status was evident in the dresses and hats they wore and the suitcases and bags they carried.

It was the late nineties and we were told that most people were struggling economically. Some teachers had not been paid for months and many families were living off of the food from their country gardens. The poorest of our guests wore wool blend and carried their belongings in multi-colored woven bags made of plastic as they arrived at the hotel. At the hotel we also saw women arrive in nice fur coats with more than one bag. I saw at least one woman with her baby in a sling wrapped warmly next to her. The story was that she had come in by train and it took two days. The forecast was normal for them for the time of year, but it was brutal for the Americans. It was a few degrees below zero.

Part of the electricity in the auditorium was the height of anticipation that we had been told about and felt prior to our arrival to the auditorium. The amount of poverty in the land and the years of being cut-off from democratic neighbors left the people hungry for something more. The expectation and hope for life giving words from a few (approximately twenty) American women seemed to border on desperation. We were treated like visiting celebrities or a strange phenomenon as we walked the streets. People would stop to stare. Some even wanted to touch my skin or hair as I was one of a few people in the group with dark skin. Some children were openly curious or repulsed at something so foreign. The older women didn't seem to care about what I looked like, they just seemed to want something. It haunted their eyes and I wasn't sure that I or we could give them what they wanted.

Thankfully, we were told ahead of time by our host that the women liked prayer and liked for religious guests to lay hands on them. This was a relief because I knew that whatever they were longing for had to come through me instead of from me. True to our church tradition at the end of a passionate message there was a call to prayer for those who wanted or needed it. They were told to come up front where members of the team waited to pray with them. I don't think any of us expected the numbers that responded. We all had a line of people that we briefly prayed with as the assigned interpreters made the connection. It seemed from nowhere a forty-something looking woman stepped up to me. I could not discern her social status from her dress or demeanor. She wore a head scarf as many did and her dress and shoes were non-descript. She spoke rapidly to the interpreter and the interpreter rapidly spoke to me after short phrases. At some point her voice began to break and she began to cry. Out of all the other women that I had rapidly prayed with, this had not happened. However, she began to tell me a heartbreaking story about her son. She told in detail of how he had become very rebellious, became addicted to drugs, and ran away from home. She didn't know where he was at the present. She wanted me to pray with her about his safety and his return home. At the time I was a young therapist who had worked in group homes most of my young career. I had probably talked to hundreds of parents about their rebellious teens. I didn't have a teen at home, but I felt like I had mothered quite a few. I did have a toddler son that I had left at home to come on this trip. There was something about her story that roused in me every bit of motherly instinct that I had ever been given in my lifetime. All of a sudden I could see her son lost somewhere and I could feel her pain as she had watched him go. I understood the crazy worry of not knowing where he was now. I started to cry with her. I started crying out to God with an urgency as if we could see her son in the room. I started telling God what we needed and what we felt from a place in my gut, and not from my head. I don't even know if the interpreter could understand what I was saying because I was speaking so urgently, so passionately, in a language of the heart and not of the mind. Understanding or not, the interpreter began to cry and the woman totally convulsed into sobs as the three of us clung to each other. In those few moments, the external world disappeared. No longer were we in Moscow, no longer was I a Black American, I was just one with this woman and her pain. Then the next phase of the supernatural happened that I don't have words to explain. It was like the electricity in the room had become a vacuum around us that engulfed us into a place of love and security. When our tears stopped, we were all smiling. She was thanking me profusely which felt weird because I had done nothing extraordinary. She expressed feeling satisfied and looked quite peaceful. I too felt her peace that had become a bow that tied us to each other.

Although I had done nothing extraordinary, the encounter was extraordinary. Not because of who she was or her issue or my identity, but because I saw her. I mean really saw her and felt her pain. I couldn't have conjured up or mentally worked out this sense of peace for her. Yet, I believe because I was open to all of it, my past experience, her present state, and both of us being desperate for the supernatural, it somehow happened. The same power that transported her to a place of peace left me with wonder. It felt good to be a part of that transformative experience, but I wondered how I could be open enough to have this happen again? That, along with other experiences, transformed me in a way that left me often looking for the supernatural in my encounters with others. I no longer wanted to depend totally on my skills, education, talent, and natural resources. I knew that each worthy encounter had the potential for something so much more.

MEDITATIVE EXERCISE:

In a prayerful stance (whatever that looks like for you: sitting, standing, kneeling, or lying down), pray for someone for whom you choose to make intercession. Allow your imagination to picture them in color. For example, what would the person be wearing? Hear that person's voice in your head. Say whatever words come to your mind, heart, or mouth as a prayer out loud. Be sure to write about your experience.

Chapter Four

Hope: Life's Greatest Weapon

It was a cloudy and rainy day like no other when I received the phone call that one of my former clients had died. She struggled with depression and anxiety much of her life. She used recreational drugs to self-medicate and sometimes tried to escape by some form of attempted suicide. Once particular time involved a gun to her head. I was called that day too. I even sat with her one day in a padded room in a nearby hospital while the medical professionals decided if she would be admitted. Each time I talked with her or met her, above my counseling training, the best thing I had to offer her was hope. I spouted psychological principles, affirmed her pain, offered interventions, but most often prayed with her. It was in the times that I prayed that I saw the inner her and the spirit that could, would, and did endure. I could feel the demons of her past fighting me even as I prayed, but I could also hear and feel the God of the present saying pray on and that she would live and not die.

We were as different as night and day: culturally, in stature, in the way we were raised, the side of town we were from, and ideology, but we met around one thing: the pain of living and the hope of continuing in a life with purpose and joy. She would suddenly stop coming to therapy without explanation only to return again months later to pick up where she had left off. I would lose touch with her because she moved around a great deal and there were always new addresses and phone numbers. Funny thing was, she would always find me over the years. No matter where my new office was located, she would find me. For years she would find me. Then for years there was no contact, until one day out of the blue I got another phone call. She said that she just wanted me to know that she was on a good path and life was good. She wanted to thank me for all the years of help. She was sober, connected to friends, and spiritually rooted. She sounded better than I had ever heard her sound. I was thrilled. It seemed that all of those hope interventions had found a place of sustainability. I knew that this wouldn't mean that like in some fairytale she was living life without imperfections. However, I knew that she was now living life with some purpose. Even better, her phone call instead of showing up at my door meant that she had found a way to generate hope internally.

Two weeks later, I got the last phone call, the one from a friend who said she had died in her sleep the previous morning. No drugs, no sickness, no struggle. She had peacefully gone to sleep. The friend said, "she would want you to know." I did want to know. However, I struggled with how to sum it all up. Her life that had such impact on a young therapist trying to offer something to someone who was really struggling with life. Years later, I have come to believe that my greatest lesson from this encounter is that hope is the greatest weapon we have in the fight against the darkness, evil, self-doubt, fatigue, sickness, loneliness, failures, etc. If I experienced any sadness, it was connected to the fact that she left this life too soon. However, her legacy will be the story of her tenacity and strength to keep moving despite the weights that try so easily to beset us.

She obviously learned what she needed to make it through the times of struggle. One of those things was a strong support system that included me. This network was there to catch her when she was falling and hold her arms up in prayer when she was weak. I knew her family that was praying and supporting her in other ways. Another part of her support system was her church. I would encourage her to go even when she didn't feel like it. She would report back of feeling the energy from others by just sitting in the sanctuary. There were times that she reported feeling that the pastor was talking directly to her giving her God's answers to her prayers. This was obviously through divine intervention because she would have never told the pastor about the depth of her struggle.

Through counseling she learned the power of addiction and strategies to resist zoning out. She also learned the power of childhood trauma in adult life and the stronger power of the process of forgiveness of self and others. In this process she was able to let go of unhealthy relationships and learned how to recognize healthy ones. Hope may seem like an intangible or philosophical concept, but it has very tangible results. It is the partnering in a life like this lady's that makes me feel purposeful and hopeful in the midst of each challenge.

MEDITATIVE EXERCISE:

Take a few minutes to remember a difficult time in your life. Who and what gave you hope that life would get better? Be specific and write them down. Tuck the list away in an accessible place so that you can pull it out when you need to use it.

Chapter Five

Casting Your Fear

Philippians 4:6

By definition, anxiety is the activation of one's fight or flight response, usually due to some external or internal perceived threat. Fear should tell us something either about our environment or ourselves. Granted, sometimes the fear turns into panic and is not helpful. This is when the fear totally overrides our rational thinking and being. We go into a sustained automatic response that is not healthy. Something or someone has to jolt us out of this response.

She was tearing the cabin apart. Pulling things off shelves, undoing beds, knocking over well packed baskets, and at times brandishing a piece of wood as a weapon. She was a fifteen-year-old Black female from the worst streets of Atlanta. She was at least fifteen pounds heavier and a good foot taller than I was. She had seen more degradation and manipulation in her fifteen years than I would ever see in my lifetime. We were in an outdoor camp deep in the woods of Georgia. A camp established by a church with the theory of having a practical mission.

We had built our own cabin out of mosquito netting, pine trees, and canvas. This was a major part of the therapy program. We had learned how to cook our food when the camp cook was not present, sometimes by campfire. I was in charge of ten girls.

My mission was to help them therapeutically transform their angry, rebellious natures into something that society and their families could tolerate. They had been brought here because other facilities would not take them or because they had been failed by those facilities. Some had been in and out of foster homes most of their short lives. Their parents most often were looking for drastic measures to institute drastic change. One condition of the placement was that there had to be a relative or substitute willing to work with them while in care and be a placement after the course of treatment.

The biggest problem was that many of these girls had major trauma histories and most of their reactions were out of fear and anxiety that manifested as either murky depression or all-encompassing fireball anger. In this instance we were getting the later. The cause of the scene that I was encountering could be something as little as a spate with a fellow bunkmate or as major as a letter from home with bad news. It was probably a combination of the two.

It is important to note that the weapons of my scholastic skills and training consisted of an English Education degree, weeks of on-the-job training, and what I thought was divine calling. The latter is what gave me the most skill, along with skills learned growing up in my family of eleven. This was before any psychological training except for Psychology 101 during my undergrad. The first level of training in this type of atmosphere consists of one learning how to deal with one's fear and anxiety. If you respond to fear or anxiety of others with uncontrolled fear and anxiety, all is lost and usually more trauma is the result instead of any therapeutic measure.

Maintaining one's wits is paramount. It doesn't matter that the person in front of you is holding a weapon, calling you foul names, and threatening to permanently maim anyone who comes close. Another lesson learned quickly is that though these threats are in anger, they will often tried to be carried out. Again, handling fear and anxiety is paramount, second only to allowing your rational mind to stay in control and relax enough so that your spiritual nature has room to work. You see, it is not that one is not afraid or anxious because the threat is very real, it really is about how to handle the fear and anxiety so you know what to do or not to do with the threat.

I had worked hard to establish a trustful, respectful, and kind relationships with each one of the girls in my group. Each was unique and it was important to acknowledge each person's uniqueness. Their learned ways of coping even during calm and routine days was totally fascinating. Majoring in these different coping styles was another lesson in survival and the ultimate in learning to teach and mentor. Most girls were responsive and flowered under steady, consistent unconditional love, boundaries, well thought out consequences, and a bucket load of understanding through conversations.

The moment of showdown was how all of this would show up in the fireball encounter. She (the fifteen-year-old) made her way to the bathhouse creating havoc in her wake. She cussed, screamed, and threw things left and right as she walked. The rest of the group had learned how to manage their own anxiety for the most part during such episodes. Depending on the length of stay, some hid until the worst was over, some took advantage of the situation by going to find something they wanted, and most others simply followed looking on trying to figure out what good or bad things they could learn. I watched and followed praying and hoping her anger would just fade with time. I tried several times to talk to her. She responded with more threats. The real moment of truth came when she started directly for me with her weapon. Looking back, I'm not exactly sure what stopped the big stick from connecting with my head. However, it seemed that things happened in slow motion as I saw it coming at me. I called her name as if it was a prayer. I also remember feeling a supernatural calm. I stood my ground. I did not run towards her or away from her. That seems important in hindsight. I would like to think that in that breath prayer what she heard was the months of understanding, awareness, and my trying to love her. I would also like to think that my nonjudgmental compassion and anointed presence meant something. Maybe it was all of that and something more, but it stopped her in her tracks. She suddenly became calmer. She was not totally back to baseline, but at least calm enough that I could convince her of reasonable actions.

I learned more about unconditional love in the years that I worked at this camp than just about any other place in my life, with the exception of marriage. There is a psychological theory that suggests that one who learns to sit with his or her anxiety (fear) is the one who will grow the most in any relationship.

MEDITATIVE EXERCISE:

Write about the last incident in which you felt a great deal of anxiety and/or fear. Allow yourself to experience the fear and ask yourself why does this make me anxious and/or what is this fear trying to tell me? Imagine yourself sitting in the presence of God. What are some solutions that come to you to address the fear that you were facing? Write down what comes to you.

Stretch a little more and tell a trusted friend about what you discovered.

Chapter Six

Hospitality as a Key to Resiliency

We had been riding for hours when our guide told us that we were stopping. We were leery and weary; it had been a long day. MJ, an archeologist and our instructor for the trip, could talk for hours about a rock in the road. We had been on the journey since early morning and had seen beautiful things that day and eaten lunch in a cute coffee shop in the middle of somewhere in Lebanon. We were told that members of the Hezbollah came calling there at times. Now here we were stopping in what looked like a very dusty campground with houses made of what looked like mud beehives. By the way, the camp looked to be in the middle of nowhere. Our local guide got off the bus first to greet our host who came to meet the big bus that seemed so out of place. We were a group of seminary students and businesspeople from America who were more than curious about all of the people groups of the Middle East. MJ was a research professor at heart and loved the countries of the Middle East and probably knew more about the rocks there than the average native person. The women and children were the ones who came out of a home to greet us. They stared curiously but had hospitality on their lips and in their eyes.

We were offered tea and it was a chance to use an outdoor potty. The women on the bus would have made the tea for the chance to use a potty that didn't stink as bad as some that we had used in the past. This one was outside so how bad could it be?

All twenty of us were ushered inside the tent after our potty break. The furniture was sparce and so were any signs of prosperity. We took the small cups of tea with gratitude as we sat crowded on the mud brick floor. We knew better than to refuse. However, the conversation through an interpreter was so much better than the tea. We heard bits and pieces of the family's story of having been pushed out of their home and homeland. The war had brought so much devastation. What war it was became muddled to me. I was so enraptured by the resilience and the hospitality of these people in the middle of nowhere in a hut with a dried mud floor. We all sat there trying to hang on to every word and wrap our brains around how so many people could be displaced from their homes. Who was going to save them? How were they going to eat for the next few days or months?

I had grown up poor and knew what it was like to live in a ragged house with little to eat. I had experienced poverty of identity as well as possessions. What I was having a hard time understanding was the fact that these people did not seem to have a government aid program or the Red Cross or a church outreach ready to provide resources. Maybe they were there and we didn't have time to find out how it worked, but there was no evidence of any of that in what we saw around us for miles.

I know the adults had to be concerned and there was some concern in their words. However, there were no tears or pleas for help or even for a donation. They simply told their story and invited us into their world. The energy of love and family connection was in the little hut. The few things were set cozily about. There didn't seem to be disarray in the mismatched pieces on the floor and walls. There was a certain order that they must have established in their lives while living on the edge of emptiness. It didn't take much to imagine them in a home even in America with a white fence with flowers around a nice wood or brick home. In the essence of the relationship there was no difference in what I would have experienced with one of my neighbors on my street. Tea on the dried mud floor in Lebanon or Syria (I don't know which) felt very much like talking to my neighbor at her fence. While hoping and praying for a way out for them, I couldn't help but pray that I have this much grace and hospitality when I encounter chaos in my own life. The visages of who this family is went far beyond their last name or even their nationality. Their countenance just said neighbor full of hope of some kind and offering hospitality out of that. I really hoped that I could be this open when my life was this broken. You see, I know that my natural inclination is distrust and to close up. My natural inclination is to preserve what I have and not share so quickly in a time of scarcity. My natural inclination is to be embarrassed, even ashamed when visitors come by at what I don't have instead of proudly offering what I do have. It is often too easy for me to see the mud, sparseness, and taste the bitterness of tea. I have to really work at embracing the mismatched creature comforts and holding lightly the teacup. The key is remembering just some of what they showed me. One important lesson that comes to me is the affirmation of the simple concept that we need each other to survive, not because of the financial or material resources, although those certainly are needed, but at the basic level we need each other's perspective of the world. We need each other's caring presence and listening ear. We need each other's will to live and acceptance that we all are dying. We need each other's touch in a way that says there is something bigger than individual existence. We all need the comfort of sitting with someone who is truly interested in our individual stories. This kind of hospitality surely can lead to acceptance and healing.

MEDITATIVE EXERCISE:

Decide in this moment that today you will find someone you believe to be very different from you to invite into your space. This could be having a cup of coffee together on a break or inviting someone to lunch. A really daring move might be to invite someone you don't know very well over to your home for a meal. Make the appointment today while the inclination is fresh.

After the event, be sure to write about all that came up for you: thoughts, feelings, and awkward moments. Write especially about the negative feelings and try to figure out the why.

Chapter Seven

Enlarging the Narrative

She was a prisoner and I was a minute part of the prison administration. That was supposed to make us enemies. From what I had seen of the way the system worked, prisoners and those who work in the prison could at best establish a truce that enabled a working relationship. No one trusted anyone. I was there on a mission. I was a chaplain student with many years of experience as a therapist and some years as a pastor. I was still young enough to be naïve about what I had to offer the world and believed that my brand of faith could overcome any obstacles. The strict rules that moved with the wind, endless body counting, and constant search for contraband carried out by a militaristic style of leadership seemed hard on everyone. It seemed hardest for the women who had the "audacity" to commit a crime and get locked up while pregnant.

I met this particular young lady while conducting a bi-weekly spirituality group. It was voluntary and open to all of the pregnant women in the small prison. There was never more than ten to fifteen at one time. Over time the group shrunk to five or six and sometimes one. She was the one. She came originally because her entire block wanted something to do to pass the time. The first time she sat silent with an angry demeanor that didn't quite reach her eyes. Subsequently, she would maintain the angry demeanor but started to ask questions. Usually she would follow up my answer with an answer of her own. Her answers seemed to contain a mixture of different religious philosophies. Most of it was garnered from authors from African descent, most of whom I had never heard their names. She seemed strong-willed and very opinionated. However, as the group shrunk in size, she shared more of her story. It was filled with abuse, trauma, and a lot of illegal decision making. She never made excuses for her decisions or expressed any real sorrow about the abuse despite the tears at my calling it out. Eventually we acquired a mutual respect for each other. She called herself an atheist and I made no bones about the fact that I was a Christian, but I didn't apply any pressure to her. We each talked about what we believed, why, and how it connected to our circumstances. Early on it became evident that she believed in God but didn't know what to call God and was still looking for answers to many of her questions. Her life seemed to be filled with so much pain as evidenced by her story of a suicide attempt. She wanted so much for the baby growing inside her that was soon to be delivered while she was trying to grow up inside a prison.

I am unsure when this young woman began to change my life, but I began to see my mission as something different from what I originally thought. I was no longer just a chaplain in a seemingly crazy prison system, but a human being trying to figure out how to express the love and care of God without using simplistic outdated language, but rather simplistic dialogue that would give hope and purpose greater than the present circumstances. I suddenly had lots of questions about how to be intensely present in an intensely uncomfortable situation with lots of barriers.

The day of ultimate test came for both of us as I found out from another staff member that she had been taken to the hospital for an emergency delivery. This was the beginning of a nightmare that all of the women often talked about. They expressed concern about the level of care that they would receive if ever they had problems with their pregnancies. Their ever-present distrust of the system was full blown when it came to their medical care. I was never sure what to believe when they talked about the medical staff and what they saw as below standard service.

When I presented my request to see her in the hospital, it was treated with disdain by the powers in place. It took employing a great deal of prayer, maybe some fasting, and finding the right person who would re-interpret the rule book to allow me to make a one-time visit. When I got to the hospital everything looked like a normal hospital ward until I got to her room. There was a security person at the door in full uniform. Inside she was in the hospital bed with a metal restraint on her leg cuffed to the bed. She looked awful. Her gown was askew, her hair was matted, and her face was a mask of sorrow as if she had just seen death at its worst. Her baby was alive, but she couldn't see it at the present. She knew that the baby had suffered some type of illness and would have an ongoing defect. She would eventually be shipped to a prison and a family member would have to take the baby. As she answered my questions, the anger she normally wore was mixed with bitterness and sadness. When I asked if I could pray, she did not refuse. I was told that I could not touch her and the security officer scrutinized us closely. I do not remember what I said, but I fought not to cry. The last thing she needed to handle was my sorrow. I do remember trying to convey love to her. I felt it stronger for her than most human beings I knew in that moment. It was bigger than me and not coming from me. I hoped that it was radiating from me as I could not voice it or touch her. I think she felt it. At the end of the prayer, I saw the tears in her eyes as I blessed her future and never lost eye contact. Then, I slowly turned and walked away. We both knew that we would never see each other again. I hope and pray that the narrative of her life has been as enlarged as mine has been by our interactions.

MEDITATIVE EXERCISE:

Make note of when you will find a day to volunteer in a facility where the occupants have limited access to resources. Set up the appointment before the day ends. On the day of service, make a point to talk to people and keep an open mind about the stories or partial stories that you hear. Be sure to be internally prayerful during these interactions. Please don't naively try to fix anyone or the situations you encounter.

At the end of the day or the next day write about the following: What was a surprise to you? What was expected? Does it make you view people differently? How? Why?

Chapter Eight

The Messy Process of Faith

It was three o'clock in the morning and there was a knock on the door. Just like he said. I'm not sure I slept at all, although my roommate and I went to bed early with the pretense that we would get good sleep for the journey ahead. Our guide for our Middle East adventure told us that we would traverse the mountain in the darkness so that we could see the sun rise over Mount Sinai. I kept asking myself why this was so important. The tour guide/ professor who was to become a spiritual guide really didn't give me a sufficient answer. He simply said something like, "It was something that everyone should experience." I really didn't think much of sunrises and sunsets until this man became my tutor. He seemed to think there was something special about them. He often made a point on the three-week tour to take the group to a place where we could see it rise or set.

We were all excited about being at Mt. Sinai, the place where man met God according to sacred texts of major religions. The red clay looking mountain wasn't what I expected. It wasn't necessarily scary among the other mountains in the range. We could look at its majestic presence from a hill across from St. Catherine's Cathedral which sat at the foot of the natural sculpture. It was neither menacing nor inviting, just a sight to be taken in and interpreted as one contemplated and reflected on its place in history. The goal was for us to climb the approximately four-mile trip by camel most of the way and walk the last mile or so. I had never ridden a camel in my life. The idea of riding up a steep mountain pass in the dark made me more than a little nervous.

We arrived at our starting destination. Of course, it was dark. The anxiety of the anticipation had mostly subsided into excitement. The voices all around me said the same about my group companions. Our tour guide gave a few instructions about the journey. He said that our camel driver would do all the work. There would be a pause at the rendezvous point. We could possibly get water and walk the rest of the way.

The path where the camels and drivers waited for us was lit only by the building lights nearby and maybe a few flashlights. My first issue was getting onto the camel. The camel driver was nice enough although he spoke no English. Nor did I understand whatever instructions he was gibbering at me. The reigns were fashioned around the head like on a horse. The difference was that the camel driver led from the front on foot and pulled the camel along. The saddle seemed to be at least six feet up and I am barely five feet tall. My foot kept eluding the stirrup that would give me the needed lift to hoist myself up to the high hump of the camel. It took quite a bit of awkward lifting, pushing, and shoving on my back side to finally got me there.

Once I was perched atop the camel, I immediately wanted to get down. I could not imagine sitting precariously atop this tall animal that would be moving up a steep incline. I felt like I was in a tree. It seemed ludicrous and I wanted to scream for help, especially as I heard my group moving away from me. For some reason, the flashlights were turned off as we started moving and the darkness seemed darker. The lit buildings were now behind us. I felt rising panic and tried to tell the camel driver that I needed to get down. After finally getting is attention, I motioned my need to get off. He frantically shook his head no and fired off something in his native tongue. This was problematic, as we spent a few precious minutes arguing in different languages. Meanwhile, I had no idea where I was in relation to the other group members. I am a counselor and therapist, so I know how to calm myself. I took some deep breaths and assessed the situation. I prayed nervously. I was unsure that I expected God to answer, but I prayed mostly out of habit and desperation. I decided for that moment it was best to just keep moving. So, we did.

The next problem was that the more we moved, the higher the elevation. Yes, I know that is how mountains work, but atop a camel it seemed that I was leaving the ground behind and levitating in mid-air. Instead of wasting time arguing with the camel driver, I decided it was time to jump down. After all I could just walk four miles uphill, right? Once I hit the ground hard, the camel driver turned and started a tirade of gibberish. He gestured wildly with his hands which mostly meant get back on the camel immediately. I just kept shaking my head no. Strangely enough, I was not afraid of this brown-skinned, dusty man in baggy clothes with his head covered in cultural garb. As a matter of fact, I was somewhat indignant at his now commanding attitude. Actually, I think my fear had just taken control and I was acting out of pure emotion.

Thankfully, he did not leave me. He and camel walked beside me. Maybe this was God answering my prayer. All I know is that after probably not even a half of a mile I was exhausted from trying to walk in what felt like quicksand up a hill. It was time to surrender. I was frustrated but knew that now was the time to really just trust that God was in the process and that I was going to get where I needed to go despite my fear. So, I humbly and somewhat ashamedly asked the driver in gestures to help me back onto the camel. He actually seemed relieved to do so. After once again awkwardly hoisting me back in place, he took his place at the reigns. I was near tears as this time. I fervently prayed about my fear of being so high up, about feeling separated from my group, and feeling stupid about arguing with the camel driver. Once I came out of the stupor of my self- pity, I noticed the silence of the night and the brightness of the stars in the sky. All of a sudden, I remembered my favorite Christmas carol. "Silent night, holy night, all is calm, all is bright. Round yon virgin mother and child. Holy infant so tender and mild. Sleep in heavenly peace. Sleep in heavenly peace."

I had sung that carol since I was a child. It always felt comforting to me and brought back all the goodness of Christmas memories. My attention then went back to the stars that seemed to be winking at me. As we climbed the mountain, they seemed to get closer and closer. I was no longer afraid because they somehow brought me comfort. I thanked God for being with me as we trudged onward the rest of the journey.

When we reached the rendezvous point, there was a makeshift open shelter that had hot tea. My comrades were there conversing about the journey to that point as they waited for each group member and camel driver. Funny thing, of the ten group members, each person had a tale about the trial in learning how to ride a camel up the mountainside. As a group, we were able to laugh about the angst, excitement, joy, and pure triumph. Out there seemingly alone, it was simply a lesson in learning to lean into trusting the process of the journey.

MEDITATIVE EXERCISE:

I invite you to spend some time alone sitting in a dark room. In the initial few minutes of total darkness, what do you feel? As your eyes adjust to the dark, where does your focus go and why?

What does God have to say to you through this exercise?

Chapter Nine

Appreciating the Grace in Lostness

It felt like a dream as I gazed out of the bedroom window at the Parisian street below. How did I get here from a small town in South Georgia to looking out of a hotel window in one of the most loved cities in the world. My roommate brought me back to reality. Our room was tiny; barely big enough for the two of us to turn around in with one bed that we would share that night. It was ok though because we were in Paris. She was wondering what we would do about lunch and what was next on the agenda. Thankfully, there was no real agenda. We had spent several hard days in the winter of Russia. We had an assignment there that was full of agendas and food that we struggled to get down at times. It made the sunshine streaming through the window even more sublime and the little streetside cafés look more inviting. We had no idea what the rest of our group was doing as the group had split for individual entertainment.

I suggested we explore the city. My mode of operation for travel was to read a travel guide or take a tour to find the hotspots in the city. However, as often is the case, we didn't have our own mode of transportation. Even if we did, neither of us could speak, read, or write the language. I had taken French in high school about twenty years prior and wasn't even sure if I could pronounce bonjour appropriately. Out on the busy street things looked as they would in any other big city. Cars passed us on brick layered streets where we stood, pedestrians passed looking preoccupied, and the shops looked as though they were preparing for business. A check of our watches for the appropriate time (sometimes confusing when crossing continents) told us it was near lunch time. We decided to try something near us because we were hungry. We also only had twenty-four hours in Paris as technically it was a layover from our flight home. We passed a few cafés trying to find one that might be kind to a couple of hungry, yet not French savvy, Americans. We found one in which the person standing at the door with a white chef-looking garment greeted us with a smile. When we told him we didn't speak French, he tried to help us in halting English. The first sign of incredible grace in a foreign land! His friendly enthusiastic manner convinced us to take a seat and menu. With gestures and his halting English, we were able to order and eat a wonderful fish lunch.

Hunger now satisfied, we were a little more adventurous. We decided to take one of the tour buses like one would see in New York with seats on top of the bus. We couldn't understand the commentary but we did get a guidebook that had some English. Atop the bus we were awed by the postcard like image of the Eiffel Tower, transfixed by the historic architecture in the business district, and mystified by the Arc de Triomphe. The latter we didn't have a clue about, but its imposing majestic presence drew us in. We were like little girls basking in the beautiful culture and chattered away about what we saw. For just a little while it was as if we were in a fantastic wonderland drunk on the sights and sounds of the city. It was like the little girl in a scene from The Nutcracker. The cars, buildings, and people danced around us while we bent and twisted to try to take it all in. There was no real processing of historical facts or even geographical location. No one even looked at us as if we were foreigners like they had in Russia. Looking back, it never occurred to either one of us that we might get lost because we were totally filled with the joy of being in that place. For the little while of that tour, I experienced and understood the concept of total childlike wonder. The city was as delightful as everything that I had read or seen on television.

It wasn't until the bus reached its destination and we had to descend with the other passengers did we realize that we didn't know where we were in relation to the hotel. It was 2001 and cell phones were not as common. There was no way to contact our companions or even call the hotel for possible transport. We had managed to take a business card from the hotel. I'm not sure this was strategic on our part or just part of the grace of the adventure. We did the first thing that came to mind out of instinct. We started trying to ask people passing us about the location of the hotel. Once we started explaining ourselves in English, people would shake their heads or wave us off. A couple used a short French phrase in a tone that felt like they were saying, "Get the bleep bleep away from me."

At that point I started to feel my anxiety rise and found it mirrored in my friend's face. She started shortening the ask by stopping people to inquire if they spoke English. In return we still got the quick shake of the head without barely a pause in their steps. I found myself at an interesting internal place when I had to acknowledge to myself that we really were physically lost in a big city that was thousands of miles from home. We couldn't speak the language, didn't have transportation, and didn't know a soul who could help us. It didn't help that hours had passed and we knew we didn't have long before darkness descended. I knew that I could either give way to panic or use the resources of my past to do what I could do. This included praying silently and quickly. We finally had the marvelous idea of hailing a taxi and showing him our hotel address. He was able to get us close enough to our street that we were able to use a street map to find our hotel.

It has occurred to me that it took a real balancing act to enjoy the fullness of our little adventure. It took relying on our practical skills, spiritual intervention, partnership, past experience, and emotional intelligence to navigate our journey. However, it also took fully giving in to the wonder of the experience to get the greatest joy out of what our surroundings had to offer. I know that I am sometimes too much of a thinker to enjoy the ride and what God is offering. This adventure helps me to remember that there is so much joy in the journey if I can just allow myself to relax and get lost for a time.

MEDITATIVE EXERCISE:

Please allow yourself to go for a drive today or sometime soon and get lost on a country road for a few miles. Enjoy the scenery and hear what God is saying.

____

____

Chapter Ten

Becoming Like Little Children

The directions that I had been given told me that I should turn off the nice, paved highway onto the muddy dirt path in front of me. It didn't seem right because I had a hard time believing that any house could be at the end of such a narrow, almost overgrown path. I had to avoid some holes and uncovered rocks which made the drive a bit bumpy. The mud, all of the mud, seemed to be thing that was most disturbing. I was in the middle of a lull in the rain that had been present for a few hours. Finally, after several minutes and probably only a mile, I came to a clearing. There was more space, but still a lot of mud. There was very little grass, but many houses in the clearing. I use the word house loosely. The structures looked like they were barely standing. The one closest to me was supposed to be the house of my client. It looked as though it was put together with only a few nails and maybe some glue. The plywood looked rather flimsy and I'm not sure what type of material composed the roof. There was smoke coming out of a chimney. This made sense since it was a bit chilly for late October in Georgia. I could actually smell the smoke in the air. I asked someone passing by about the house of the client for whom I was looking. The passerby confirmed that my eleven-year-old client lived in the house with the chimney smoke.

I pulled my car close, and with my umbrella along with a note pad in hand, made my way to the door. There wasn't a step or stoop or porch in sight, just a door. A very frail looking woman opened the door just a crack. Her bones seemed to be jutting through her skin with no excess fat. Her dark skin looked wrinkled and dry, although I knew she had to be in her forties. "Ms. Emm, I'm Betty Williams. I know your son from school," I spat out rapidly before she could close the door in my face.

She looked as if she might, but didn't. "What do you want?" she mumbled back.

"I was wondering if I could talk to you about Jimmy? I'm really concerned..." I started to say, but my words trailed off.

She wordlessly opened the door a little wider and allowed me in out of the chill and misting rain that started again. The room was incredibly hot from a wood stove in the middle of the room that seemed to be the extent of the house. There were two or three other adults sprawled about the room that was sparsely furnished. Jimmy was nowhere to be seen. There was a small tv that captured everyone's attention until I walked in the door. All eyes turned to me at the point. Suddenly, I felt so out of place and wondered what I was really doing there. I had only seen her eleven-year-old son four, maybe five times, at the school. I had been assigned to him by my director at the local mental health clinic. He had been referred by the principal because of his chronic oppositional behavior in the classroom. When I set out on this journey thirty minutes after the school day ended, I felt like I had every right to confront the mother of this young child. After all, I was the expert about to graduate with my counseling degree, but here I was standing in the middle of this little house feeling like a naive little girl who needed much more understanding and training. The mostly male audience behind Ms. Emm looked very experienced and maybe worn out by life. Their clothes along with her clothes looked smoke stained and dirty. I had known poverty growing up, but not this kind of poverty. To stand in the middle of it was gut wrenching. It was also very humbling. I felt if they wanted to do so they could chop me into little pieces verbally and psychologically. I summoned my big girl courage. I turned my back on the other adults and lowered my voice. It had the desired effect of creating some privacy as the others went back to the tv. This time I verbally reached for the understanding from her that I needed. "Ms. Emm, I need your help. I am the counselor assigned to Jimmy to help improve his behavior in the classroom."

She immediately looked defensive and said that she was doing what she could to keep him on track. I asked about his daily activities after school. She assured me that she made him do his homework when he got off the bus. She said that he went to a friend's house after that almost every day. This really sounded like a cover-up. I had learned some things directly from Jimmy. When he came to his first counseling session with his too big clothes and sullen silence, he would only shake his head yes or no to my myriad of questions. I learned to use another tactic. To my utter amazement, he began to respond to my sessions of coloring on the floor. After hauling in my sketch pads, markers, pencils, and crayons, I learned that he liked to draw pictures. This had opened a world of short sentences that helped me to piece together a partial picture of his story. What I heard was a little boy who hung with older boys after school. The things that they did were bordered on being illegal and sometimes garnered money. He would sometimes mention certain colors being important which made me suspect gang affiliation. There were often casual mentions of violence. I knew pretty quickly that I wasn't going to get very much from the mom. However, I did warn her that I thought Jimmy might be involved in a gang and that his safety may be an issue. I knew immediately that this was not news to her. She gave an answer that she thought would satisfy me. In the end, I climbed back in my car feeling like I had been the one schooled that day.

When I returned to the school a few days later, I was met by an administrator who told me that I would no longer be seeing Jimmy. When I asked why, I was told that his teacher was furious with me. Upon further inquiry, I was informed that although Jimmy's antagonistic behavior had improved, he would no longer sit in a desk. He simply wanted to sit on the floor and draw pictures. I was shocked...why would this teacher not see the absolute necessity of my continued work with this child. The floor play, in my mind, was his entrance into really becoming a child again instead of a "little man" struggling in an adult world. Well, the teacher wouldn't talk directly to me, the principal wouldn't defend me, and my supervisor gave up trying. If only I had the words to make them understand how taking on the characteristics of innocent children helps us all with transformation. If I had been able to find the words or some key, I might have helped save a child's life. I can only hope and pray that there was some other intervention started by my intervention that took him to the next level of transformation.

MEDITATIVE EXERCISE:

Find an object, a song, or a piece of artwork from your childhood and allow this thing to connect you to your identity as a child by touching the object, looking at the artwork intensely, or listening carefully to the song. What positive characteristics can your garner from this experience to bring into your adult life? Don't forget to write down your thoughts and feelings.

Chapter Eleven

Mothering

She was over the stove in her favorite place in the house when I encountered her for the first time that day. The house was big, old, and cold, yet full of comfort and love. The kitchen smelled of soup and the wafting scent felt like a big warm hug on a cold day. It was all symbolic of who she was. When I was a grad student, new mom, and new wife, Peppy adopted me. She played the role of therapist, career mentor, and spiritual director for the young struggling me. On this particular day, she was my safe place away from the storm that was occurring in my life. Only a little while ago she was on the floor playing with my toddler complete with a toy train and using her character voice to read to him. I didn't even understand how one person could care so much about people that she barely knew. That was Peppy! She was often feeding someone, taking in someone off the street, and/or adopting a needy person. She was also a social worker, community activist, and sojourner for truth in many forms.

I had come to her a couple of days ago running from life. She allowed me to sleep in her spare room and wanted to cook for me until my head stopped spinning. That day was significant because I would have to make some major life decisions. I was at a fork in the road. Taking the wrong path could mean total destruction for my career and be a detriment to my son. To take the right path meant that I would need lots of guidance and resources. As we sat at her big oak table and discussed all the pros and cons, she was the epitome of presence. Peppy didn't get angry or shout, but she showed much emotion at my times of stubborn naive thinking. She didn't laugh at my silly notions that were too big for me, but simply smiled and reframed them in a way that I could grasp a smaller goal. When I reached an impasse of pain she simply sat and waited me out. When I had spiritual questions, she didn't pretend to know the answers. As a matter of fact, she never wore her spirituality on her sleeve, yet it was so much a part of her that you couldn't miss it. Her holiness could easily call out my sometimes pretentious and guarded nature. After a few days in her humble abode, I knew which road I would take. She helped me connect to the needed resources and continually supported me through the emotional roller coaster.

After muttering through this catastrophic time in my life, I was overly impressed with this idea of mothering. This idea of connecting to a female figure who was unrelated but could offer all of the powerful benefits of a biological mother. I find it interesting maybe even strange that I didn't see much of Peppy over the years after this major fork. We would sometimes run into each other on the street. We would hug, laugh, and talk about the work we did together at different organizations. We would renew our commitment to one another and promise to be intentional about our next meeting. Unfortunately, we never did. However, there is no mistake about the fact that she made a mark on my life.

It is one thing to love someone unconditionally but quite another to be able to activate that love in an impactful life changing way. That is what I consider "mothering." There is an intuitive gift that is encompassed in the act. One has to know the other beyond physical contact. There is a knowing of a person's past and future that can be seen simply because of life maturity, care, and God calling. There is a way that the mothering one passes on wisdom that makes it more than just information. Often times the receiver may not even be ready for the gift. However, it has a way of sticking with the intended recipient so that when it is needed, it comes up again.

There have been a precious few mothering women in my life somewhat like Peppy, but not exactly like her. I am appreciative of all of these women; they are in my DNA somehow. When I look back over my life there were at least one or two who were part of my childhood and growing up years. There was an elementary school teacher who read Bible stories to her class every day. What I most remember about her is that she would allow different students to sit next to her during group time. When any one of us did something well, she would give us a special squeeze or hug that went far beyond any type of grade. When she looked into my eyes I felt like she saw my soul which was beyond my skin color, clothing, or the insecurity of a country Black girl. She bought me things not out of pity, but they seemed to come from this place of motherly pride. She never told anyone or asked for any credit. It was like she knew that I needed things and wanted me to have them because they made us all look better. She appeared periodically throughout my academic life. She would be there to affirm and to cheer me on to greatness. It is from her that I learned the gift of how to cheer on others.

There was also the pastor's wife who represented every church lady that I have ever known. She was special though in that she could be every woman but still be herself. She exuded a comedic strength that didn't care what other people thought of her. She had a way of getting what she wanted while making others feel that they were being more spiritual by giving it to her. Despite this, you had to love her because she had an easy laugh and a hug that enveloped every trouble you ever had. She could make fun of any situation and only waved her hand at hard work. Yet, she got lots of things done and supported her man. She had a way of making you feel loved while kicking you in the backside with a verbal punch. I think I may have tried to steal this particular knack from her.

I give tribute to these beautiful women here because they filled in certain holes in my life. They never took the place of my biological mother but they were present in her absence and gave when she couldn't. They never criticized her but in some ways spiritually stood beside her. As I take my place as an elder in the circle of life, I can so appreciate the ways in which they make me who I am. My hope is that there are some young women in my life who will remember some mothering that they received from me and my footprints will be a part of their journeys.

MEDITATIVE EXERCISE:

Go on a journey of finding photos of women who have mothered you in your life. Find a space for looking at those photos and remembering how their personalities touched you and transformed your life. Write it down.

____

____

Chapter Twelve

My Sister's Keeper

I can still hear her in my dreams. She was screaming, "Please listen to me! I am a woman! I am human! SEE ME!!"

It was hard to hear her because she was buried in an ancient institution that held a million different stereotypes. I was working in that system which told people when to move, be still, lay down, get up, and often what to believe. I knew that when I took the job. It was supposed to be a part of their rehabilitation, right? I was there to make a difference. With my lofty ideas and pre-established goals, I was going to help save someone.

I met her during orientation. We were trained not to ask why the women were being locked away or how long they had to stay. However, all of them were quick to tell you. I was assigned the duty of spiritual orientation which meant I was to read the book about what chaplains had to offer those behind prison walls. Even in this, I tried to be as humane as possible and talk real about the rules as they became acclimated to a step-down facility that was still in many respects a prison. She was much like all the other women who came through, except that she had a different look of consternation and her questions were a little deeper. Our conversations took on a quality that felt like life or death. She had a loyalty to her religion as a Muslim that went further than jail house escape.

The tests started the day she told me that she was fasting during Ramadan. She had come to the conclusion that she needed to wear her hijab as she felt spiritually convicted about not doing so. She came to me, the appointed institution chaplain, because she had addressed these issues with the administration and had been denied. What was she supposed to do now? I felt this was a good question, but I didn't know the answer. So, what does one do when one has no idea what the rules are in a rule-oriented institution? One consults the rule book.

After consulting the rule book, I found that she was well within her rights to wear religious clothing and follow religious tradition as long as they did conflict with the safety of the facility. Then the turmoil set in. I, as a Christian, would begin this fight with administration about the rights of this woman, my sister, right? When one is in an institution where no one and nothing is trusted, one has to be very careful and prayerful about how one addresses the administration. One could easily find oneself the enemy of the state.

After much prayer from both of us and submitting requests to speak to the right officials, I was allowed to briefly make intercession. My presenting of the rule book was not received well, but it could not be denied. I was told by the woman after some "reprimanding language," she was allowed to wear her hijab. I was also intermittently given some "reprimanding language" about how not to allow myself to be taken advantage of by the imprisoned.

The real test came the day that the woman requested that she be allowed to attend a mosque. This request was not illegal because there were Christian organizations that were busing women to their place of worship from the facility. It is important to note that over the months prior to this request, I had gotten to know the woman well. She would come for counseling and we would talk about her lost family, broken relationships, and her deep convictions. We cried together, laughed together, prayed together, and traversed theology together. I found myself day and night in classes with professors, having conversations with peers, and wrestling with this idea of how what I believed connected with what I was doing in relationships with the diverse group of women that I was trying to serve. The question generated from Cain's question to God in Genesis 4:10 kept coming back to me: "Am I my sister's keeper?"

The answer always came back with a resounding yes! Yes, I am my sister's keeper.

The next part of the journey was writing letters, making phone calls, and asking permission from the powers of administration to move heaven and earth to allow this sister to have transportation to travel back and forth to a mosque. After making contact with an Imam who was familiar with the facility, we were able to get her request granted in accordance with rules of the facility and the proper conduct of the woman.

The backdrop of the story is that I often felt like I was choosing to stand for justice in a system in which justice was often delayed, denied, or sometimes covered up. I also felt like I had to deny some of the theology of my peers and of my youth to choose to be sisters with someone of a different religion. After hearing differing opinions, reading the rules, discussing the theology, and really consulting God's presence, it all came down to this for me: God really did have the final say so. This woman's faith felt real and God was in the process, so what more was there to do?

The moral of the story for me was how engaging a system and someone different from myself can be a catalyst for transformation. Though we do not keep in touch and I never saw her again after she left the facility, I will always remember my Muslim sister. Mostly because we connected in a deep sense in a moment in time that was not expected and in a system that seemed to be full of expectations. I know this is true of most human established systems. I now find myself looking beyond the rules and the expectations to see what supernatural encounters might exist that can change lives.

MEDITATIVE EXERCISE:

What are the systems in which you frequently engage? Think about one person in a system who is most different from you and write a letter to that person (not to be given to the person).

Start with the questions you might ask and allow your letter to progress to something meaningful you might say. Be sure to ask God to be a part of this process with you.

Chapter Thirteen

Fresh Fire

I grew up many miles away from the interstate. What interstate? Any interstate in Georgia. Dusty roads and pine trees were more of what made up my surroundings than asphalt roads or brick buildings. The murmur of the wind, buzzing of mosquitoes, and the smell of fresh tobacco on the stalk during the summer months was more of what I was used to as a child. Life was slow and fairly simple, consisting mostly of work with family, recreation with family, and church with family. Church, in my mind, was the social event of the week. You dressed in your best and got to see everyone in the neighborhood. This was exciting because otherwise, the family who lived next to us was at least two or three miles away. On special Sundays we had dinner on the grounds which meant that my mom had cooked for the last twenty-four hours along with other relatives. The church we attended was very small and was surrounded by a few scattered houses. The church was a simple, wooden one-room structure. In the center was a raised pulpit that few dared to trespass. Around it the saints gathered to pray on Sunday mornings and Wednesday nights. In front of the altar sat a communion table that was also sacred, but doubled as other things when the elders gave permission.

I grew up attending this church. I think my mom took me as a baby. My grandparents attended that church, several of my aunts, cousins, sisters, brothers, etc., attended that church. Matter of fact, most everyone I knew who went to church went to that particular church. I was used to hearing hymns being raised by the deacons and one pastor or another preaching fire and brimstone sweaty sermons. On a really good day with good attendance, you could hear the stomping of shoes on the wood floor and rhythmic clapping from the church yard as someone wore out an emotional verse. On other days it was just the mundane of going through the motions of Sunday School, preaching, Wednesday night Bible study, and socializing before and after.

If I had to pinpoint a turning point, I would have to say that it germinated with an experience on a hot summer day in our unairconditioned house in the country. I must have been around twelve or thirteen years old. A book, really a pamphlet, that belonged to my sister that had been lying around the house for days suddenly caught my attention. It wasn't until I was a few paragraphs in that I realized that it was religious material. As I began to read, the room melted into the background and the words seemed to burn in my head. I was arrested by this interesting notion that life could be eternal. Included in this concept was this idea that my life somehow needed to be different and *needed to make a difference*. Suddenly I had this mental vision of fire. It wasn't consuming anything, but it seemed to be tangible. The flames held a slow rising heat that made my skin glow with warmth. My insides were full as my bones radiated the heat. I felt tearful yet not quite sure why. The fire disappeared as quickly as it came. The experience only lasted a few minutes, but the effects lasted a lifetime. I knew that it was supernatural and that I would never be able to articulate it to anybody. This writing is my first attempt at trying.

The next Sunday morning during the altar call and "opening of the doors of the church," I didn't see the fire again, but I started to feel the same internal warmth. I began to sweat and felt like crying. This time it was a prompting to do something, like get up and go to that altar. Was this God? I tried to tell God all the reasons why this was not a good idea. I began with the fact that I was too young. It didn't seem to matter because I found myself moving toward the preacher on wobbly legs. When I got to him I was so nervous I could barely speak. I could have sworn I heard my siblings, maybe even my mom, laughing and telling me to sit down. If they were, the reverend ignored them and seemed so pleased that he laughed and hugged me tight before taking me through the rituals.

I know it sounds like a cliché, but from that day forward my life changed. I felt like I could I do things that I couldn't do before. For example, prior to that day my sister knew how to push the right buttons to make me so mad with her. We often fought like sworn enemies. After that day I learned how to allow my anger to subside and speak to her with kindness. It was like I suddenly became smarter in school. I seemed to know things that I had not previously known. Even at church I began to read the Bible out loud and teach others. No, I didn't become superhuman, but I did become more aware of life; like there was another dimension to life that I had not previously known. I had stepped into that dimension. The more I studied, prayed, and learned, the hungrier I became.

The songs of church became ways to intimately connect to God. I no longer tried to tune out the deacons' garbled poetic prayers or ageless hymns; I began to imitate them with a passion. I became more curious about the inner workings of church. Things like business meetings, Sunday School, and the church calendar. Things that bored others became important to me. The most fascinating part was the response of others to my enthusiasm. In indescribable ways, my change, although it seemed strange to those around me, changed their attitudes and behaviors toward me. No longer was I just the fifteenth child in the clan who was muted in the background, but I suddenly had a voice that would be heard.

You may read this as simply the awakening of a pre-teen girl to adulthood in general, but what if it wasn't that simple? What if there really was something supernatural at work that could be activated in all of our lives? I mean, what if everyone could become aware of another dimension of life that started a fire that changed them and their surroundings? Isn't it worth asking the question?

MEDITATIVE EXERCISE:

Look back over the last thirty days of your life: were there small supernatural happenings that perhaps you ignored or excused away? What if those happenings were God calling and those happenings were an invitation to step into something different? Allow yourself a few minutes to imagine what a more exciting, passionate, engaged life might look like. Write it down.

Chapter Fourteen

Run for Your Life

My husband and I were sitting in wing seats at the beginning of what was supposed to be something like a twenty-hour flight home from Monrovia, Liberia. He was nearest the window, but I could see the wing of the airplane and the runway as we started to ascend. Once we were in the air, I could see the beautiful blue of the sky with whiffs of white clouds. My beautiful view was abruptly interrupted by a flash of something passing the window. My husband and I jumped, startled by the fire sparks that came next and the black smoke that followed. We looked at each other wordlessly as the plane did something weird. The look spoke volumes with questions at the center: What just happened? Are we going to die? What now?

Thankfully, the plane did not immediately drop from the air, but slowly descended back to the ground. As it was coming to a slow roll, the pilot was telling the three hundred passengers that there was an engine issue and we needed to sit tight while he figured out what happened. The crowd on the airbus was eerily silent as we all waited to find out what would happen next.

I tried to look back to see where the rest of my team was seated, but I only spotted two of the four. They looked as perplexed as everyone else. It was 2008 and international cell phones were not as popular, so there was no texting each other. As for my husband and I, we were strangely calm as we wondered what had happened and what would be the next move. I was most interested in getting off the plane. I had heard too many stories and seen too many movies where the wrecked vehicle bursts into flames. My backpack that I always used as a carryon was under my seat. I had already started to pray, and this would only intensify.

After countless minutes, we could see that the plane door was being opened along with other maneuvers being performed. One stewardess finally grabbed a mic to address the group. She spoke rapidly but fairly calmly in two different languages that we didn't understand. When she finally got to halting English, the only thing I remember her saying is *"Run for your life."* Now, prior to this, no one who heard in the other languages seemed to be moving. Even after hearing this in English very few people moved out of their seats. Those who did simply stood in the aisles. I'd watched enough movies to know that one should not panic and make crazy moves in these situations, but it did not make sense to me that people were *not* moving. I looked back at my husband, picked up my backpack, and readied myself to move into the aisle. It turned out that I had to excuse myself past people in order to get to the door of the plane. It was like watching a movie and the people were either moving in slow motion or were stuck in a still frame.

Looking back on it I can only surmise that the majority of people were in shock or really didn't believe that the situation was dire. I, on the other hand, felt the gut instinct to survive. I was praying for the team that we would all get out of this alive. I was also remembering the prayers prior to this journey and the distinct promise from God that though our lives would be in danger we would win! It wasn't until I got to the door of the plane that I realized the enormous size of the plane. The jump to the ground looked about fifteen feet with only a half-inflated safety raft between me and the end result. In the best circumstances, one was supposed to jump onto the raft and slid to the ground. While other people stood contemplating the jump, I took a deep breath, knowing my husband wouldn't hesitate, and jumped. Though the raft cushioned the force of the jump, there was not enough air for a comforting slide to the ground. It was more like a crawl to the end of the raft with the help of others who had gone prior to my descent.

When my feet hit the dirt, I began to run. My instinct was survival; to get away from the plane in case of fire. You see, running for my life was not something strange for me. The gut level training from childhood trauma, the years of doing spiritual warfare inside and outside of non-profits and religious institutions, the pulling of others out of dark holes, and the learning to love unconditionally had made me very aware that there were times when you must run! Sometimes running is not the simplest thing, but *the most important thing*. Sometimes running may seem selfish or cowardly, yet necessary. In the running you know that you have to eventually face what is behind you, but in the moment of a fight or flight decision, you sometimes just need to run.

We live in a culture that perpetually tells us to fight, stand your ground, don't give up, etc. In this culture, those messages are the messages of winning. However, it was in spiritual attunement that I knew that my winning was in the running. It brings to mind the wisdom of the writer of Ecclesiastes, "the *fastest* runner does not always win the race; the *strongest* soldier does not always win the battle..." (ERV 9:11). Just stay attuned enough to know when to run! I was not interested in outrunning anyone else that day; I simply wanted to survive.

No, the plane didn't blow up and yes we eventually arrived home safely, but the lesson in running lives on. I've often talked with people who refuse to quit or walk away from something toxic because they believe that somehow there is shame and no glory in staying until things blow up. However, those who are willing to let go of external voices and listen to their spiritual gut are typically able to know when to run for life and find more abundant living.

MEDITATIVE EXERCISE:

Time for a gut check: What decision have you been wrestling with over the past week, month, year? Stop wrestling with all the pros and cons of the voices around you. In a quiet place, listen for your voice, and listen for God's voice. Are there places of letting go that would make the journey easier, more holy, healthier? Let go and run...

Chapter Fifteen

Spiritual Warfare as a Means of Growth

There had been rumors of a teenager levitating in chanted "prayer" after bedtime and strange things were seen moving around his room and around the cottage. His admittance to the program had caused quite a stir among the patrons as well as the administration. He was one of those who barely met the criteria for our in-patient mental/emotional/behavioral rehabilitation program. It was not for those who were likely to run, be violent, or approaching the legal age of eighteen. His paperwork read like someone had seen the boundaries and made sure his history just missed the mark. Despite this, failing numbers to meet budget and state interests helped the administration make the decision to take him. However, after a week of disturbing things happening in the cottage with no one else to blame, the administration began to think differently.

As for my part, I was the assigned therapist and my job was to gather history, find out the issues we could work on as a team, and write the treatment plan. Sounds easy enough, and in most cases it was. However, just sitting with this patron for an hour was not going to prove easy. I had heard all of the rumors and had read his file thoroughly. My research even included calling his caseworker. So, I knew how many foster homes and institutions he had been released (kicked out) from. The last home had been unique and his longest stay to date. They were devout Christian people and reportedly had seen a remarkable positive change in the teenager. This was true until one day everything changed. They began to see a rapid decline until a blow-up happened one night that resulted in the police being called and ultimately a placement at our institution was necessary.

Our one and only meeting felt like a showdown of sorts. I came armed with all of my information and the goal of being the savvy therapist who would find out who this teenager really was and hopefully find ways to help him before he reached full adulthood. What really happened was the teenager told me of a tragic journey that led him to one bad decision after another and challenged my spiritual maturity. He expressed no remorse about his exploits or his engagements with the dark world. As a matter of fact, he bragged about them. When I challenged him about the lies he had swallowed along the way, he turned red with anger. Eventually he was so angry that his face turned into a red inscrutable evil twist, complete with teeth that looked as if they had been sharpened into spikes. At the same time, he raised his razor-sharp fingernails so that I could see them.

He never threatened to physically hurt me, but in a low, chilling, throaty voice challenged who I was as a Christian. As I prayed out loud in his presence, he challenged the validation of my prayers. When he told me his assumed name from the dark world, he very confidently acted as though he knew me. The strangest thing was that I believed him, and I still do. I believe that he knew me as the person who loved God and had served God most of my life.

I believe that he knew me as one who practiced spiritual gifts and spiritual disciplines regularly and lived a life trying to serve God while trying to serve others. It was a strange sensation that a person who was representing evil with every fiber of his being knew the spiritual me.

As scary as that was in the moment, it was incredibly reassuring because if he could so completely embrace evil yet still know me as a child of God, then I could be very confident that I could access everything that was God's. It also meant that despite what he was saying, my prayers had incredible power and he knew it! Having that knowledge made me more confident in my prayers and I verbally reached for the little boy that looked like a young man ensconced in the lies of evil. Eventually the soul of the injured teenager came back into the room. I can't even really say that I won the battle that day or that I made some indelible impact on the scarred teenager. He was eventually shipped from our facility and on to the next institution. The only thing I know for sure, based on that encounter along with others in my life, is that spiritual warfare is real.

If we, as Christians, believe in a supernatural God then we must believe that there is more to life than what we can see, hear, or touch in the natural realm. Having that knowledge makes me frequently question how this should impact the way that I live life. How many things do I/we miss in the day-to-day world that are influenced by the supernatural? How do I access supernatural power and how does that make a difference in the lives of others? The young man I described used the power of evil to intimidate and sometimes hurt others. He admitted harnessing the power of evil to gain things, hurt people, and escape consquences. So what does that mean for us as Christians?

Can we access the power of God for God's glory and for the good of self and others? In the spirit of Ephesians 6: 10-20, how much of what we are struggling with in this world is really about what is evil? How then should this inform our fight?

MEDITATIVE EXERCISE:

Read Ephesians 6:10-20 very slowly. Pray, then read it again. What lessions are in this for you?

Write them down.

Chapter Sixteen

Redefining Safety: Upside Down

As a teenager and pre-teen, being anywhere with my pastor was the safest place I knew to be. He had been a mentor, teacher, cheerleader, and spiritual role model. I loved him like a surrogate father. It was nothing for me to jump in the car with him to go on a journey. I was delighted to be his front seat partner even when others refused to go. Usually it meant going to church in a nearby small town and sometimes a stop at a local store for a treat. However, one particular night at the beginning of such a jaunt, we were in for a tragic surprise.

It was very dark on a country tree-covered road not far from my home. It was during a comfortable pause in our drive time conversation that my pastor suddenly stomped on the brake while muttering an exclamation under his breath. It jerked me forward as I too began squinting into the windshield of murky darkness, beyond the dimmed headlights, wondering what had caused such a reaction. Other than feeling things slamming together, I don't remember much movement after that, and things went even darker.

I woke up some time after, minutes or maybe hours. My eyes

were open, but still not seeing much. I remember feeling myself upside down in the car which was possibly leaning to one side. I kept trying to move in an effort to right myself without much success. When I finally managed to fully open my eyes and see, I saw my pastor slumped over the wheel. There was crying or maybe muffled screams coming from somewhere. I found myself trying again to get to that person. I needed to help, but couldn't seem to move. Sometime later, minutes or maybe hours, I found myself in the back of ambulance speeding to a hospital.

Many pieces of the story of that scary night didn't come together until days later. There are some pieces I have never known and will never know. It turned out there were deer hunters, for whatever reason, parked in the middle of the road with no lights on as we rounded curve. We did slam into them and unfortunately one person died. Thankfully, everyone in our car came out alive. However, I have a facial scar to this day to help me remember the night of slamming into a windshield and turning my world upside down for just a bit.

I happened to know the daughter of the person who died that night. She was a friend and a classmate. It is hard to describe the emotional turmoil during the first twenty-four hours of finding this out and coming to terms with it in a small town. The biggest surprise for me was the love and compassion that I received from this friend despite the negativity that we received from many and the grief that she experienced at the loss of her father. She and I really got to know each other in a different way at another level. There were surprises of love and support that came from others as well. The journey of healing the ugly facial scar and my self-esteem is another miracle story that needs to be told at another time.

However, the safety points of this story are worth writing about. I never had hard feelings toward my pastor or felt unsafe riding with him after the accident. As a matter of fact, he continued to be all that he had been up to the day he died. It wasn't until years later in a therapeutic session that I realized how much God's protection had been an incredible factor that night and all through my healing journey. This may sound strange, but often when I thought of that night I would think of my pastor's care who represented God for me, and how safe I felt with him even in the midst of the crazy parts of my journey. However, as a part of a hypnotic session, I was asked to relive the incident and talk about a lesson from the reliving of it.

Well, the biggest learning for me was that I hadn't remembered that a person that I did not know rescued me from the car that night. As I understand it, the car was turned sideways in a ditch which was the reason I was upside down. In reliving the story, I remembered a male rescuer opening the car door and reaching in to get me. He took me into his arms and carried me to safety. For some reason, this imagery was such a powerful picture of God's love for me. It was even bigger than the picture of the father figure whom I had known most of my life. This somehow made the definition of safety more poignant for my present-day life because it said to me that God would rescue me from any situation and that he was not bound by time, space, or a physical body.

This reminds me of the paraphrased words of the Apostle Paul in Romans 8:37-39: "I am convinced that nothing can separate me from the love of God." The miracles that I experienced in the process of healing was further proof of that. This included the forgiveness and deeper friendship of my classmate and the other joy giving surprises along the way that far outweighed the suffering in the tragedy. Unfortunately, it sometimes takes traumatic incidents or extreme stress in our lives for us to see through our basic theological concepts and/or our adopted religious ideas to greater truths. I do not have theology for the the death of my friend's father that night but on these pages I am choosing to focus on the truth of what I know of God's love and the safety of that for me.

MEDITATIVE EXERCISE:

Make an appointment with a trusted friend, spiritual mentor, or trained counselor (someone safe) to process a story of a time of challenge in your journey. Be intentional about verbalizing the theological and/or spiritual lessons learned from this telling of the story. Remember to write down these learnings.

Chapter Seventeen

Pride and Prejudice

I didn't know if I should cry or rail in anger about the injustice of the story that had just been told to me. I stood in the counselor's office of my small high school in my small hometown. The teller of the story happened to be a Jewish man who came from a Northern state and found his way to this population. This was probably because of similar situations in similar small towns that made him want to help smart young naïve Black girls like me.

If the powers in place knew that he was telling me the story he probably would have lost his job or at the very least been reprimanded. He knew this and was telling me anyway. Looking back, I'm proud of this man that I barely knew. He was telling me the story of how the award that I had won based on academic achievement and leadership abilities shown on paper was being taken away because the sponsors, an all-white male organization, found out that the student that they were sponsoring was a black girl. The award included a trip that would help the recipient in finding a college education and help the candidate enhance his/her leadership skills. My counselor had nominated me not only because I met the requirements, but because he knew that I needed much impetus to get me to college. He encouraged me to use all of my talent and skills in the world to come but knew that I needed a college degree to get me where I needed to go. While telling me of the obstacle, he also confidently told me that we would overcome it. He assured me that he would find another organization that would sponsor me financially. This probably meant making contact with organizations out of my county and making the case for my worthiness. So why was he telling me the back story? He could have done the legwork without telling me or taking the risk.

My counselor knew that I would have to do this kind of legwork for much of my life and was proving to be the role model that I needed. Somehow, he knew that I needed to know that he believed in me to bolster my self-esteem enough to fight for my seat at the table no matter what arena I found myself in. He knew that I would have to work harder than most and that the struggle would build the character to allow pride about who I am and where I had come from be bigger than the prejudice that I would face.

In the time frame that it took for us to get a different sponsor, while he worked his resources, I had to work on not becoming bitter. It was probably the first time in my life that I became aware of the many acts of racism in my life since childhood. The adults in my world talked about such things, but as a naïve small-town girl, I just mistook those acts as a part of life that I would have to endure. It was the first time that I became aware that I had resources at my disposal to use as weapons of defense and a voice that could make a difference in the larger scheme of things. It came at a crucial time in my life when I was just beginning to learn what faith in God was all about.

Obviously, it didn't mean a life of Christian impact would be easy but filled with learning to forgive with eyes wide open. The tricky process of forgiveness is finding the strength to make the decision to do so then pray for the anger, sadness, and shock to subside. While prayerfully wrestling with the emotions. It is important to not make quick decisions that are hurtful to those around you. I remember thinking that surely my teachers knew what was happening and it seemed that they were complicit somehow in the injustice. Despite this, I couldn't lash out because I needed to maintain a good average and prove worthy of the goal.

I was also driven by a goal of making my family proud of me and maybe subconsciously representing my culture in a way that was acceptable and that elevated us in the eyes of our society. I did not know at the time the magnitude of prejudice in systems all over the world and the many who were fighting for cultural justice. I knew nothing about political systems and very little about religious systems but this incident for my teenage self was a prophetic vision of the incidents to come. In truth, that incident was minor compared to those that had come before and some that would come after. However, it was if having someone name it that was of a different culture and fight with me validated my perceptions and was divinely sent to say, "Here marks the line in which the way you deal with such things change." No longer was subconscious acceptance ok for the subconscious or conscious biases of others.

My counselor did find another organization to sponsor me and I did make the trip with the help of friends. It was a week of sitting with the best students from schools across Georgia. It was intimidating, but I was glad to be present at the table. In case I haven't said it enough, the whole incident prepped me for years to come. I made it to college.

MEDITATIVE EXERCISE:

Journal about an incident in your life that could have made you bitter but instead made you stronger because of the people who helped you through and the way you handled your emotions.

How might you use what you learned to help others?? Write it down.

Chapter Eighteen

Adulterated Compassion

It was a weekend night in the ER at a level one trauma center. I was the on-call chaplain whose beeper had gone off yet again. In trauma bay five was my patient with her husband sitting in a chair near her bed. He looked like he had been in a fight. He appeared to be in his late fifties or early sixties, as did his wife. His hair was mussed, clothes were dirty, and there were remnants of blood on his shirt. Actually, they had been in a car accident. His wife lay in the bed wearing a neck brace. She was in a hospital gown and covered by a sheet. I could see a view bruises and scratches, but no other obvious injuries. Two young female nurses stood at the other side of her bed. I assumed one was reading test results while another busied herself with medicine machinations. I could only hear snatches of their whispered conversation, but based on what I could hear, slow movements, and glances at the patient, things were not as serious as they first appeared.

It was when the bed started to violently shake that we all startled to attention with all eyes going to the patient. She was staring at the ceiling and shaking from head to toe. One of the nurses rushed over, put a hand on her, and said in a normal voice, "You are going to be ok. Your tests are fine."

The shaking only paused and began again so violently that the bed rattled and could be heard through the thin walls. Her husband tried next. His voice was not gentle, but at room volume and he called her by name, "Louise, they say you are going to be ok."

Louise did not verbally respond and continued to stare at the ceiling. She did stop shaking for a few minutes, but started again as soon as her husband sat back in his chair. Next, the same nurse found a blanket to put over her and said more loudly, "YOU ARE OK! We are going to get you fixed up and you can go home. YOU ARE OK!"

The bed continued to shake violently with her body tremors. Husband got up again and in his outside voice said, "LOUISE! YOU ARE OK.! STOP SHAKING" He sounded annoyed, embarrassed, and was ordering her to stop immediately. Louise looked startled. Her face had the expression of a cowering animal who had been kicked while scared, yet her body did not stop shaking.

As chaplain I am trained to intervene only when appropriate to do so. I'm supposed to allow room for the medical team to do their jobs. Even though I look like I am doing nothing, I am assessing the situation and praying. This last episode of trying to calm the patient convinced me that it was time to intervene. I stepped forward and said, "Please let me try." After getting within eye space, I leaned down in a soft voice to speak to her. "Mrs. Jones, I am Betty, the hospital chaplain. You are in the ER and the nurses are taking care of your medical needs. You are going to be fine. Just listen to my voice." I held her hand and continued, "Just breathe slow and try to relax. Deep breath in, deep breath out."

She followed my commands and maintained eye contact with me. "That's great. Just relax." I felt her hand respond to my hand. "Yes, you are going to be fine. Just breathe. Soon you are going to be able to go home." She nodded and I stayed with them until things seemed under control.

This episode was significant for me because I walked away wanting to teach people how to respond to others in crisis. It was evident that both the nurse and husband wanted to help Louise, but they each responded to her from a place of intense emotional energy and did not have enough compassionate energy to respond in a way that was needed. I can imagine that the nurse was responding out of her fatigue from the overloaded night in a frantic ER. Her training was to help people physically get better, not mentally/emotionally. Perhaps it did not occur to her that the physical reaction that she was seeing was from a mental/ emotional state that needed addressing. Another hypothesis is that maybe she did see that the couple needed emotional support and knew that she did not have what it would take to deal with them, so that is why I was called. The husband, on the other hand, seemed depleted of compassion by the trauma of the night or did not have the emotional intelligence to know how to hold another when in crisis.

So, what was the takeaway for me? We are only as strong in a crisis as we are in how we do daily self-care and stress management. Honing our spiritual disciplines, coping skills, and relationship management skills need to be an intentional part of everyday living. They help us in getting through each day and they are automatically in place when we need them most if they are a regular part of our daily routine. We cannot have genuine care for others if we do not have genuine care for ourselves. Love God with everything you've got, then love everybody else like you love you. That is my own interpretation of Matthew 22:37-39.

MEDITATIVE EXERCISE:

Doing good self-reflection is the beginning of honing all of the above skills-hence the reason for these exercises. Take a few minutes to make a list of spiritual disciplines and coping skills that you employ daily. Next, write a list of the people who are a part of your support network. When was the last time you called these people?

Chapter Nineteen

The Power of Praise

He sang in the airport, he sang on the bus, and he sang in the shower. He also sang at the most important times in our lives. In the best of times I think it would be putting it lightly to say that my friend was not the lead soloist in the choir. However, it really doesn't stop him from praising God through song. Obviously one of the spiritual disciplines of our Liberian Mission team member and friend is singing. On the trip, we all teased him about the fact that he seemed to know only one song. It went something like this: *"How great is our God, sing with me, how great is our God."* A few words taken from a song made popular by Chris Tomlin.

The words of that song were tested over and over again during the Liberian journey. It probably was tested most for Alex during his bout with a sickness a few days into our journey. We knew he was scary sick the day he could not sing because he could barely hold his head up due to the fatigue, nausea, fever, and chills. Probably out of former Marine stubbornness he stayed with the team although he should have stayed in bed. The medical person among us, my husband, supplied him with medication and we diligently prayed. I believe that it was his love and worship of God that got him through the hardest days and the spiritual reserve that got him through the worst day. Once his fever broke and he was on the mend again, he began to sing again.

What Alex may not have known was that the song that he sang over and over again in our presence actually got into our spirits. Looking back, I wonder how much of the praise and worship prep helped us on the clinic day that we were melting in the sweltering heat and overwhelming sickness. It was also the day that we danced with the villagers. I wonder how much of this praise and worship prep helped us wait hours on a van while the medical part of our team haggled with a pharmacist about the medicines we needed for our clinic. It was also the day we worshipped on the beach as the sun went down. I wonder how much this praise and worship prep helped us when we each took turns getting a stomach virus and had a hard time eating the food. Yet, we still had a wonderful servant cook who sang in the kitchen and seemed to enjoy being with us. I wonder how much the praise and worship prep helped our medical team get through the sheer numbers that threatened to overwhelm us that first day. Yet, the clinical team of two worked with few breaks all day and the next day God sent reinforcement from a nearby hospital.

I don't have to wonder how much that worship prep helped us the day we had to jump from a crippled plane. Because once we got back to the airport, our team sang this same song softly as a group as hundreds of people milled around us. *"How great is our God. Sing with me how great is our God. I want the world to see how great is our God."* The overall vibe in the airport was one of anxiety and leftover fear, but still we sang, *"How great is our God. Sing with me how great is our God."*

The airline actually opened the bar so that passengers could get a calming drink. Yet we were still singing. I later learned that the airline hired crisis counselors to help some of the passengers process the incident that enabled them with the ability to get back on a plane to fly home. As a crisis counselor, I was very impressed and grateful that some had this benefit. However, we did not, but still we sang.

It was the residual praise and constant prayer that got us through the next few days of navigating travel home. We had to spend the night in a city with no luggage, endure hour long lines to talk to travel agents to figure out how we were going to get home, and eventually had to split our group up to get tickets back to the United States. If Alex or any of us had known the adversity that we would have to endure on this trip, I don't know if one or all would have chosen not to go. Each person on the team played incredibly important roles. Obviously, one of the roles that Alex was to play in this journey was making sure the power of praise was kept in focus. Interestingly enough, if Alex was a world class singer or a powerful praise and worship leader in our church, we may not have paid as much attention to his constant song. As it were, it is proof that all of us have a song of praise and worship to sing that can and will impact the circumstances of our lives and the lives of others. There is a wonderful story of about praise in battle that drives this point home in 2 Chronicles 20:1-22. Read it and praise on!

MEDITATIVE EXERCISE:

Find a quiet space in your home to practice praying in song. Start by playing your favorite worship song and singing along. It is important that you close your eyes and breathe slowly to begin. Focus your mental attention on God. Allow this to become an intentional practice on a daily or weekly basis. Write down the things that you notice changing on the days that you utilize this practice. At some point you will notice that you no longer need the music but will have a worship song in your heart that comes up naturally and easily.

Chapter Twenty

The Tricky Art of Presence

I think I may have learned the most from my overnight calls as hospital chaplain. Usually it helped me to know what I was made of because I had to respond in crisis mode to externals with the internals of a lifetime of emotional intelligence work.

One spring night I was awakened to respond to another crisis in the emergency room. Typically when a call comes across the chaplain beeper and when you make the initial call to staff, you get very little information about what is actually happening. You either know that you should get there stat or you have a little time to dress properly and a little while to get your "head on straight." The night mentioned above was a stat call. However, once arriving in the ER, I had to talk to several staff members to get most of the story. I was told of an accident of an older couple. They were not from Georgia but had a camper home in a familiar campground near the hospital. The wife did not make it. The husband did but was in critical condition in the trauma bay while they stabilized him. The real kicker: someone had to tell him his wife had died.

The doctor who had taken care of the wife was called away to another emergency. So guess who the team thought was the next appropriate person to tell this physically broken husband that his wife was no longer on this earth? I was told that in and out of consciousness he had been asking for her. They had delayed telling him up to this point. As a young barely experienced chaplain, I began wondering what words I could use to tell this man about his wife. What would ease the blow? Was it better to be as frank as possible? I had no answers to any of the questions he would surely have about the way she died.

As the team worked to get a hold of other family members and finish a medical procedure, I had a few minutes. I chose to go to the pastoral care office to pray, meditate, and hopefully find a book, pamphlet, or something that would help a new chaplain quickly learn how to deliver bad news. In just a few minutes, a team member called my phone to say that they were ready for me. They also found a friend who lived in the campground and was the closest thing to a family member. The team decided that the friend, who also knew more about the accident, should be the one to break the news, but I would go in with her. The friend and I first met in a little room and talked through what she knew. She was amazingly calm. She was a retired medical professional and obviously still carried the skills of crisis management.

We made it to the room of the patient. He had tubes and wires everywhere. He was bandaged from head to feet and what was seen was black and blue. The nurse assured us that the pain medication had the pain mostly under control and that he could hear us. When his friend called his name, he briefly opened his eyes. In an appropriately compassionate voice she told him what was being done and that the hospital staff was trying to get in touch with his children. The room was heavy with the question that he tried to grunt out about his wife. His friend compassionately said, "I am sorry but she did not make." She told him in a very calm voice what happened after they left the campground and how the car was crushed.

The man's body began to shake with tears that could barely be shed because he was so encased with machinery and bandages. The friend stayed for a few minutes after saying "I'm sorry" over and over, touching him where she could. It was my turn. I introduced myself as the chaplain. What does one say in such a tragic moment? Well, I was as authentically honest as I could be. I told him I could not imagine the pain that he was in and did not have the words to fix it, but I would stay as long as I thought it was helpful and pray. He somehow nonverbally agreed to my presence. So, as there were no chairs in the room, I stood near his bed and prayed. Sometimes I whispered aloud, sometimes I just spoke to God in my head. Sometimes I watched as his body shook with the tears. As I whispered prayers, he shook less until he didn't shake at all. Still I prayed. The nurses came and went until they didn't come at all. Still I prayed. Sometimes I walked away from the bed, sometimes I just stood still and prayed. At some point the nurses turned off the lights to a very dim glimmer, yet I still prayed.

I don't know how long I stayed there praying but eventually there was an incredible peace that filled the room. It came in slowly like a mist in a darkened forest with the sun rising. Except it didn't dampen things but just brought with it a sweet sense of care like a warm hug on a cold night. This presence was so much bigger and better than mine that I knew it was ok for me to leave. I said goodbye to my hurting friend whom I would never see again. In parting, I told him that I would be praying whenever I thought of him.

This happening of God's presence could have been tossed away as imagining on my part. But affirmation came a few days later. One of the ER nurse's that had been in the room early during the treatment and while I was present, very graciously and genuinely thanked me for what I did that night. I wanted to tell her that I didn't do anything really but by the emotional response that she gave me, I think she knew that something unusual happened.

Knowing how to be with others when they are hurting is often very difficult. Sometimes even when you ask, a person in crisis may not know what to tell you to do for them or how to help. Most times if we can find a way to just be in the presence of the person hurting and leave room for God to work, the creativeness of God's presence can take over. The tricky art is not to get caught up in our own feelings and not allow our need to do something miss what God is doing.

MEDITATIVE EXERCISE:

Find time and a space to remember the last time a friend sat with you in crisis. What was helpful about the person's presence? What was not helpful for you? What will carry with you in sitting with others? Write it down.

Chapter Twenty-One

To Know and be Known

This was our third marriage counseling session and we were covering the same ground. She was once again complaining about something he wasn't grasping and he was defending something she wasn't hearing. The ultimate truth of the matter is that neither was really ready to be known by the other. Her childhood trauma brought her to therapy with a longing to be loved in a way that she could not get from her parents. She was ready to leave the marriage because her dating "Casanova" had turned out to be obsessively driven to be the best in his field and perpetuate all the stereotypes that the men in his family had given him. He was totally dissatisfied with the lack of intimacy (sometimes code word for sex) in their relationship and was ready to move on to someone who was more fun and not always complaining.

As the objective listener, I prayed that I could find a way to push back the wall of their defenses so that they could really hear each other. Perhaps if there was a safe space where both parties could meet without fear of being hurt or saying the wrong thing, the pain experienced by both sides could be alleviated and they could truly get to know each other.

If he could see past her dry-cleaned dress, salon nails, perfectly pressed hair, degrees, and fatigue of motherhood then he would know that her woundedness has caused her to not trust any man. She needed to know he could show genuine love born out of priorities with God first and care of self/others a close second. If she could see past his glances at his smart watch, buzzing of his cell phone, foot tapping, and the combing of his fingers through his hair, then she would see a man who was driven to avoid his need/desire to be held, cuddled, accepted, and shown unconditional love. Instead, he was fighting not to give in to the fatigue of always having to compete in the concrete jungle of corporate America where humans eat humans for the highest dollar.

Unfortunately, if I couldn't find a way to stop the crazy cycle and help them to be still and take a reflective look inside, they would be among the many causalities of divorce. Their children would reap the devastating benefits of maybe repeating the same mistakes. For those who survived, it often took three to five sessions just for them to stop the blame game and to even be willing to listen to me. Most often, couples who had a good spiritual support system, marriage mentors, individual accountability partners, readiness to listen, true self-reflection, readiness to change, true care for the other, and a willingness to learn, made it to the other side to mentor others.

As you can see from the above list it takes more than just a feeling of being in love. Commitment to another is difficult work and a true spiritual discipline. If I could get behind the wall, I think I would say and probably have said on a number of occasions something like the following:

- Every day brings new challenges, but often times the same old problems. Forgiveness is needed daily. It means making the mental decision and having faith to believe that things will get better despite what she might be feeling in the moment; sometimes forgiving the same mistake over and over again.

- Listening is everything. Listening requires suspending judgements about what he did last year, last month, and last night just so you can tune in to what his words may or may not be saying. It means putting aside the fear that if she gets to know who you are this year, she may not like you because she married the image of who you were ten years ago. It also means responding in a way that lets him know that you heard him and believe that you are going to give him space to be heard. If you don't give him the space, then there is the need for him to pray for the courage to ask for it.
- Maybe most importantly it means setting some boundaries around what is his and what is hers. When trespasses of boundaries are made, then pray for wisdom to know what to do in a creative way that doesn't have to mimic the ways of past trauma.

Yes, the work of being known and to know another is messy yet arguably the deepest kind of love that one can experience. The sparks that come from the fire of its success can last generations. The abiding joy that comes from real intimacy can be extracted to hold others. The safe pleasure of holy sharing is a role model for society.

MEDITATIVE EXERCISE:

The only way that real intimacy can truly happen is working at time together. Set a date night/breakfast/lunch with your significant other. Be intentional about the tone of the date only being about each other's hopes, dreams, thoughts, and desires.

Journal now about how you met your significant other and the things that attracted you to this person. Be sure to mention these things during your date.

Chapter Twenty-Two

Community Re-Imagined

My cell phone rang and it was my doctor. It did not sound good. She told me that she had looked at my lab work and it was horrible. I was thirty-six weeks pregnant. My body was swollen in every possible place it could be swollen. My skin was two shades darker than it was supposed to be and my hair had been falling out for days. Periodic nausea with fatigue and body cramps was just a part of everyday living for the last six or seven months. She said in a calm voice that I needed to get to the emergency room right away. Most people hearing that may have gone into some type of speedy response. I, on the other hand, had been ordered to bed rest after my doctor's appointment earlier that day and was feeling pretty despondent. I asked her if I could wait on my husband to get home from work. She responded as long as he could get there quickly.

You see, I was thinking this trip to hospital might mean a few days stay so I might need some new hospital clothes. I called my husband to tell him what the doctor said and asked him to stop at the nearest department store to pickup some hospital clothes. He didn't seem to think this was so unusual. We arrived at the hospital two hours later after at least one other call from my doctor's nurse and a command to be on my way.

Shortly after arrival, I was told that a high-risk pregnancy specialist had been called and she needed to get the baby out as soon as possible. Many years later, my husband told me that he was told that my life was in danger. I don't remember such dire news. Neither do I remember feeling very anxious. However, there are some things that will forever stay in my memory that made me so appreciative of the people that I have in my support network.

I distinctly remember hearing my husband call his family while we were in the ER to tell them to pray. I had already called my sister prior to leaving home and knew my family was praying. My husband stayed with me throughout almost every procedure.

My doctor induced my labor. I will forever remember folding like a pretzel to receive the epidural for the medication. More importantly, I remember my doctor being intermittently present during my twelve-hour labor. She seemed a stabilizing force amid the masked medical personnel rushing around me. On one of her visits she sat by my bed eating a meal. I don't remember if it was lunch or dinner as time seemed like a mystery tunnel. She was there as my baby was naturally born and I was conscious enough to smile when she laughed at my first comment about my baby: he came out looking a dusty white color.

I will forever remember the nursing team who took care of my baby in the NICU. They became like an extension of our family as we visited with them daily. They knew much more about my baby than I did and was patient with me as I made it through the process of recovery and learned how to take care of my preemie.

It's impossible to forget when family jumps into crisis support mode. Some family drove two hours the day of delivery when I groggily greeted them but couldn't stay awake to talk to them. One sister came to stay with us after I came home with the baby to cook, clean, and just be present.

Memories of my church family before during and after makes

me smile. There were baby showers with clothes that dressed my child for months. There were covered dishes sent to our house that we couldn't even eat. There were pastoral visits and bedside flowers.

My work friends and neighbors showed up as well. They came to the hospital, they came to our home, and during the whole process gave food and gifts. Everyone had funny pregnancy stories to share and mothering advice. I will forever cherish the support.

Unfortunately, the day came when I was home alone with my preemie and my husband. Everyone went back to their routines and we had to figure out this new phase of parenthood.

As I look back at these memories of my support community, I can't help but wonder if we could figure out how to make that kind of community sharing sustainable in day to day living.

I wonder if we could figure out how to make potluck dinner among neighbors a weekly or monthly event? I wonder if we could figure out how to just call each other just to check in on a regular basis? What if medical professionals were just an extension of our daily support system that knew us by name and at least some of the details of our lives? What if sitting on someone's porch just to pass the time became the new norm again? I wonder how we could help our children know their cousins across country and the legacy stories of our grandparents and great-grandparents?

I wonder how co-workers could grow as friends and not as competitors? I wonder if our partners could take time off work and the children take time from school and we could enjoy just being together in our houses without having to go on grand vacations? I wonder if we could come home from work and not turn on any device after a meal filled with conversation about what happened during the day? What if churches had days of the congregation singing and talking to each other without musical instruments or programs or electrical back-ups or people who had to work the camera feeds?

I know some will say that this kind of imagining is just nostalgia and impossible in such a complex world of research and information. However, if each of us imagined what simplification might look like, we might get closer to having sustainable warm community interactions instead of an epidemic of loneliness, neighborhood violence, and media bullying. There is a kind of simplistic living described in Acts 2:42-47. As they were in this organic community it basically says that "many wonders and miraculous signs were happening through the apostles, and everyone felt great respect for God (Acts2:43 ERV)." Sounds worthy of imagining.

MEDITATIVE EXERCISE:

Sit for a few minutes and just imagine what simplifying your life might look like. Would it mean giving away some things or putting more people into your life? Might it mean working less or working smarter? Could it mean getting to know your next-door neighbor or sharing a meal with a friend at your home? Write it down.

____

____

____

____

____

Chapter Twenty-Three

A Third Way

I knew they were waiting for me outside of the bathroom stall. The sixteen-year-old me was trying not to panic as I visualized the two twelfth graders who had bullied me for weeks. For some reason they had decided that they didn't like me. They were always together and when I saw them in the hallways or in a classroom, they would look at me with disdain. One day I overheard them loudly talking to each other about the way I was dressed. They didn't like the fact that I was dressed up and verbalized that I had an attitude of arrogance. The truth of the matter was I couldn't find anything else to wear that morning and was trying to get to class on time.

This particular day our class for some reason had PE at the same time as their senior class. This meant we shared a locker room. I was caught in a stall changing clothes when they came in the door. Unfortunately, everyone else had left and the coaches were somewhere with a door closed. So, it was me, my thoughts, God, and them on the other side of the door. Somehow, they knew I was still present as they peaked under the stall to make sure. They also checked the rest of the locker room to make sure there were no witnesses. Sure enough, the threats started. They warned me what they would do to me when I came out. They yelled, cussed, and sounded meaner than my worst teacher. I considered my choices: I could either stay in the stall while hoping and praying that someone would deliver me or I could come out with a surprise attack and take my beating like a woman. Or perhaps... I prayed for a third way. I wasn't sure what a third way might look like.

It really meant that I would just stand in the moment and see how God would show up. However, for some reason deep down I had quiet confidence that it meant that I would be ok. You see, I think the main reason these two girls didn't like me was that they saw me as different from the other sixteen-year-olds in their sphere. The thing that made me different was my confidence in God that came from a consistent prayer life, Bible reading with meditation, and being eyewitness to miracles that God had performed in crazy circumstances. These things may have made me a little bit dangerous or perhaps even seemingly arrogant. The other truth of the matter is that I think these girls were a little emotionally intimidated by a sixteen-year-old. They were both bigger, wore fashionable clothes, always had the right hair, and hung with a certain circle. I, on the other hand, wore clothes that reflected my religious fervor, carried a lot of books that I was always intending to read, was four feet and eleven inches, weighed only a little more than my books, and although liked by most students, I pretty much hung alone or with one other person.

After moments of prayer, I slipped out of the stall and pretended not to see them. I walked to my locker and began to get the rest of my things. They stared at me with insolence like how dare I ignore them. But I did ignore them. I did not even make eye contact as they snarled their dislike and what they could and would do to me. Wordlessly and with a show of confidence that I'm not sure I felt, I put on my socks, my shoes, and gathered my books. I was not in any hurry. I then stood up and walked out of the locker room without even a glance back. Later, when I made it to class somewhat shaken, I wondered why those girls didn't just attack me. Was it all just a show to see how I would react? Did God make them see something that I didn't that scared them into not touching me? I don't know, but what I do know is from that day forward they no longer bullied me.

Now, I like teaching this concept I call the third way. It reminds me of what Jesus taught in Matthew 5:38-39: "You have heard that it was said 'An eye for an eye, and a tooth for a tooth,' But I tell you don't fight back against someone who wants to do harm to you. If they hit you on the right cheek, let them hit the other check too (ERV)."

Often times conflict, disagreement, or confusion requires being prayerfully still long enough to figure out how God will have you to respond. Usually, the two easiest ways or the most natural ways to respond are immediately apparent. However, the third way is the manifestation of God that requires one to be still in the moment to allow revelation for that specific circumstance. Shalom.

MEDITATIVE EXERCISE:

Take a few minutes to think about the last conflict that you had in your life and sit with it. Allow God to help you re-imagine the person or people with whom the conflict happened. What are you learning and/or hearing in this moment? Write it down.

____

____

Chapter Twenty-Four

Just Breathe

I could hear the patient gasping for breath from where I sat at the end of the long hospice hallway. Before I could think, my feet were running towards the room. I arrived as the nurse arrived needle in hand. It was hard to tell the age of the man lying in the rumpled sheet with the bed in the upright position. As he struggled to take another breath, his head would lift from the pillow with his face contorted in an agonized expression. The wheezing sounds made it clear that very little air was getting through. The nurse was trying to help give him some relief with whatever was in the needle. However, she was having difficulty getting to the right place to administer the medicine because of his panicky movements and labored breaths. I immediately did what I always do in times of crisis; I began to pray.

I also talked directly to the man as his name came to me. I grabbed his hand to hopefully ground him. "Mr. Brown, the nurse is going to help you by giving you some medication. However, you can help the medicine to work by calming down. Try to slow your breathing. I am right here with you. God is with you." I held his hand tightly and the man stopped gasping for breath. I could see that he was concentrating on calming his body. I began to whisper over and over, "I am with you. God is with you. I am with you. God is with you." He slowly laid his head back on the pillow and the nurse was able to get the needle into him. The struggle of overcoming the anxiety and leaning into the breathing lasted long after I went home for the day. The nursing staff gave great care as this patient went into the next stage.

This incident has stuck with me because it reminds me of the cycles of everyday life. Meaning that there are things that send us into a panic and we have to be reminded to slow our breaths and lean into what is happening instead of fighting ourselves. The stressors may not be a matter of life and death, but often try to take the life out of us. Learning to remind ourselves to breathe is a discipline. Our brains, bodies, and spirits function best when we give it rest and intentional breathing. Hopefully, it also reminds us that the giver of breath and life is always with us.

Based on my experiences, I like to think of the practice of intentional breathing as a type of meditation. It involves two parts. The first part is learning to empty your mind so that you are grounded in where you are at the moment. With eyes closed, one must put away thoughts of past happenings, what will happen, or what is going on in the environment. It means telling yourself to relax so that you can pay attention to your body in repose, your breathing, and what you are feeling internally. This can happen by just sitting for minutes or hours in a quiet space and first listening to the sounds around you and then intentionally allowing the sounds around you to fade into the background.

The way to do this is the second part of the practice. Pay attention to your breath as it goes in and out of your body. As you expend your energy to pay attention to your breath, you also work to slow your breathing down; deep breathes in and slowly blow the breaths out through your mouth, then back to normal breathing with attention to the breath moving in and out. One way to help your focus and stay grounded is to repeat one sentence that is affirming or assures you of God's presence; perhaps a sentence of a learned Bible verse. You may have to tell yourself to relax many times before you get to the point of just being still.

MEDITATIVE EXERCISE:

Schedule a time when you will follow the practice in the above paragraphs: put it on your calendar. Decide now that you will not allow anything to interfere with this scheduled time. Decide on a place right now in which you will practice the above exercise. See the place in your mind and prepare it for your scheduled time. Imagine yourself doing the practice. Make time to write about the experience.

Chapter Twenty-Five

Prophetic Dreaming

The room was already filled with chatter as I entered the huge auditorium on a large college campus. Trying to find parking had been brutal so I was late and didn't really know what the opening exercise was about. This conference was one of the highlights of the month for me. I knew that it would involve some of the brightest minds in psychology in Georgia and some of the newest research in working with adolescents and young adults. It was worth the long drive, getting lost, and problems parking just to be present. Once I found a seat and became engaged, the speakers did not disappoint. One speaker was particularly interesting because of his multi-faceted holistic approach that he was taking with troubled youth in under served areas. He talked about working with the entire family in non-traditional ways that was time intensive and team oriented. This was throwing a lot of resources at an age-old problem. I could tell that all of us were impressed and we were helping professionals from several different discipines. However, even when he talked about the success rates with this population, he didn't sound particularly proud. He had the attitude of "at least we are making a difference."

This was not as daunting as the psychiatrist who stood up at one point to address the crowd as one who had many years of experience in the field and was known as one of the best. Almost in prophetic tones, he said something like the following: “I am afraid that the treatment options that are now available are not highly successful with our most aggressive youth. We have probably not seen the worst of this population. In the coming years we will see the increase in resistant strains of mental health issues and behavioral problems among our youth.”

There was a churning in my gut as he continued to talk about the myriad of reasons why. I had been in the profession for several years and most of those years had been working with adolescents and their families. Unfortunately, I had seen my share of violent youth who had been through many placements and psychotropic regimens without a lot of success. This was before the age of weekly active shooter drills, skyrocketing suicide rates, and the incredible deficit of inpatient mental health facilities. Even though dealing with the issues of the most fragile of our youth population was difficult during my tenure as a young therapist, I couldn’t imagine the challenges that he was foreshadowing.

On the other hand, having been a Christ follower most of my life, I can’t help but to hear reverberating in my head the writer’s words put in Peter’s mouth quoting from the writing from Joel: “God says: In the last days I will pour out my Spirit on all people. Your sons and daughters will prophesy. Your young men will see visions. Your old men will have special dreams...” (Acts 2: 17-18 ERV). I am convinced that the intelligence, skills, creativity, and the bold insight of this generation is the positive side of the prophetic words from this text and the counterattack to the words spoken by the psychiatrist early in my career. This is not to say that the words of the psychiatrist are not true. I have certainly seen the acuity levels of our mental health issues increase as well as the increase in the prevalence of some diagnoses. The nightly news attests to the increase in the violence and other societal woes. However, it is helpful to emphasize the offensive. The effectiveness of advanced medications, the incredible research available due to artificial intelligence (scary but helpful), and the intricacy of personal touch resources available are incredible.

However, for the older men and women to know what to do with the dreams that are dreamed, we must stay in sync with what God is doing. We are the wisdom that this and the next generation needs to be good stewards of the prophetic gifts they have been given. More than ever our God connections are not just for us but for all those around us. Seeking God's presence isn't just for the peace of the individual's mind, but the soul of the nation. It is necessary for us to know how to navigate and/or operate the systems in our society so that we keep resources available for all, especially for the most vulnerable among us. It is necessary to help us know how to uncover our unconscious biases so that loving one another is more than a moral value that we intellectualize. Those God connections are important because it is the only way we see beyond what is in front of us, more than what is tangible, and better than what is humanly attainable. Our titles and collective resources will not further transform the succeeding generations if we cannot ground them in more than the values that our foremothers and forefathers gave us. We can only transform them if we are transformed through prophetic dreaming in the presence of a transforming God.

MEDITATIVE EXERCISE:

Write down the dreams that have stayed with you over the last few weeks or months. In prayerful silence, ask God to give you meaning for these dreams. Write down the interpretations. Who are the young people in your life that you would like to spend time with? Need to spend time with? Carve out some time in your schedule to spend some time with them-you won't regret it.

Made in the USA
Columbia, SC
14 June 2024